Living Simply

Living Simply

Delia Halverson

ABINGDON PRESS
Nashville

LIVING SIMPLY

This book is printed on recycled, acid-free paper.

Library of Congress Cataloging-in-Publication Data

Halverson, Delia Touchton.
   Living simply / Delia Halverson.
      p.   cm.
   ISBN 0-687-00777-1 (pbk : alk. paper)
   1. Simplicity—Religious aspects—Christianity.   2. Christian life.
BV4647.S48H35   1996
241'.4—dc20   95-39073
                                                   CIP

99 00 01 02 03 04 05—10 9 8 7 6 5

MANUFACTURED IN THE UNITED STATES OF AMERICA

To my husband, Sam,
who has encouraged me
for forty-three
years

Contents

Introduction 9

1. The Walk. 11
2. Shall I Take the Walk? . . . Making Decisions 17
3. Stretching . . . Centering on God 29
4. Dressing Light and Comfortably . . . Taking
   Inventory of Material Possessions. 41
5. Stepping Out . . . Evaluating Time Schedules. 51
6. Listening Along the Way . . . Staying Alert to
   Others 65
7. Observations Along the Way . . . Seeing God
   in the Ordinary. 75
8. Folks Along the Way . . . Having and Becoming
   Models and Mentors 89
9. Resting Awhile . . . Worshiping God 105
10. After the Walk . . . Looking Ahead 117

Selected Bibliography 123
Study Guide 124

Introduction

So you're looking for a change in lifestyle. Or you just need a few ideas for those stressful times in your life. You're on the way by opening this book. There is a story of a man who wanted to simplify his life. He began looking for tools to accomplish this. He decided that his life would be simple if only he had a computer to keep track of his orders at work, so he went to the office supply store. The salesclerk was happy to advise him. Before the afternoon was over, he bought not only a computer with thirty interacting software packages, a color printer, and a modem, but he also bought a fax machine, a microcassette recorder for dictation and transcription, an electronic date book, a car phone, a five drawer file cabinet, a portable file, and a complete office desking system, all to be delivered to his business the next day.

The next morning he was waiting on a customer when the delivery truck arrived. As the equipment was unloaded, the customer asked the man where he was going to put all of that equipment and who was going to operate it. The man looked around his six-by-ten-foot newsstand and said, "I guess I'll have to build an office. Do you know of a good building contractor? Maybe you can also help me find someone to operate the computer for me, because I really don't have time to learn."

It seems that everywhere we turn someone has a solution for simplifying our lives. But sometimes the solution puts more stress into our lives than we had originally!

Simplicity is a grace, because it is given to us by God. We cannot buy it. We can't hire someone else to give it to us. We can't even win it in a lottery. There is actually no way we can act in order to attain it. Simplicity stems from our attitude—our attitude toward God and that relationship with God that our attitude brings. As one of God's gracious acts, it is there for us to accept.

I can't give you all the answers on simplifying your life. In fact, I can't give you any answers. The answers for your life must come from yourself and from God. I'm still working on simplifying my own life, and I expect to continue in this exercise until I die. I can, however, give you some ideas. Perhaps you'll come up with other ideas of your own as you read this book. But more important than answers, I can prick your satisfied self into action.

In this book you'll find thoughts on making decisions and taking inventory; reflections on the ordinary things we encounter and the common folk we meet; practical suggestions for taking steps in simplifying your life; and even charts and an action plan to get you started. All through the book you will be reminded that the heart of a simplified life is to find God's direction for your life and continually return to that focus.

Be aware that God works in God's own time, and don't expect overnight results. Celebrate each act that moves you a little closer to God. Look for those opportunities to change multiplicity into simplicity, fragmentation into unification.

Chapter 1
THE WALK

Every now and then there comes a time when we must clean out a space to make room for all the things we believe important enough to store. That day came upon me, and as I dug into a drawer I discovered a tissue paper bundle. As I unwrapped the bundle, I also unwrapped a series of reflections. Before me lay a handful of dried rose petals that I had gathered last summer on a walk around a lake. I sat in the middle of the floor and fingered the petals as I recalled that morning.

To my surprise I awoke to a bright, sunny day. It had rained the night before, but today was a joy to behold! I stretched the full length of the bed, running my arms and legs along the crispness of the sheets. Then my muscles relaxed and I went limp. Such a luxury it would be to lie here and look out the window, dozing for a few more moments.

And why not? I had had a busy day yesterday, and today would be even busier. Then my conscience took over. Maybe I should get up and rush to the many demands of this day. There are never enough hours to accomplish what I set out to do anyway.

I tossed about in my bed several times, deliberating over this decision. Finally my "wiser self" convinced me to get up and go right to work. As I rolled over and sat on the edge of the bed, I began to hum, "Oh, What a Beautiful Mornin'."

Yes, it was a beautiful day . . . too beautiful to pass up! The decision was made, and it wasn't to sleep or to work. God's day was calling me. I simply must get out and walk around the lake.

I hurried to the closet to select my clothing. I needed something light and comfortable, something that fit well but didn't bind when I walked. One of those special walking outfits would be nice, but surely I had clothing that would serve as well.

Dressed in shorts and a shirt, I slipped into my shoes and began some stretching exercises. Without stretching exercises, I ran the risk of muscle cramps that would spoil my walk. Proper preparation reaps full benefits.

As I stepped outside the door a whiff of freshness reminded me of a freshly washed world, now hung out to dry. Every blade of grass glistened with a fresh wetness. Such an artistic creator God is! God could have made the world without a need for showers. But God gave us the renewing freshness, with waters from on high. I sensed a new spirit welling up inside me.

When I reached the lake there were several persons already making their way along the walkway. I fell in behind them, trying to match my steps to theirs. But no matter how fast I moved my legs, the others seemed to pull out ahead of me. Then suddenly I remembered what a friend had once told me. She reminded me that we are all made differently, some with shorter legs and some with longer legs; therefore we all walk at a different pace. However, she also suggested that I could increase my own speed by reaching my legs farther out instead of trying to pound the pavement faster! As I concentrated on my body and on reaching out with each step, I began to appreciate my individual stride. It felt right! All parts of my body were working together, and they moved with a purpose.

As I came across the footbridge I heard the chatter of ducks swimming along the shore. I stopped for a moment to watch the mother duck gently nudge a wayward duckling, keeping it close by. Then I began to hear all sorts of sounds: a mockingbird's song from a nearby telephone pole, and the loud, dry rattle of a kingfisher as he dipped across the lake. Behind me, footsteps pounded across the footbridge I'd just crossed, and a frog echoed and splashed into a pool of rainwater. How had I missed these sounds earlier? I had been so bound up in my own thoughts that I missed all that was happening around me!

When I moved back on the walkway I almost ran into a young woman wearing earphones. I spoke a greeting to her, but she didn't hear me and seemed to be unaware that I was there. She too was missing the delightful sounds of the morning. As I moved on around the lake I made a point to keep my eyes and ears open.

My walk now took me between the lake and a road. So many things to observe! Like my life, the world is filled to the brim with signs of God.

A mound of vines caught my eye. At closer view I recognized the mound to be a garage, dug into the hill and now almost concealed from view by the vines. The door of the garage was narrow, evidently considered adequate when it was first built, but now far too small for our larger cars. Pieces of flat rock paved the drive in front of the garage, and dandelions filled the cracks between the rocks. White puff balls balanced on the stalks over each plant. As I walked on beside the lake I mused over why we consider some plants weeds and others flowers.

Above the vine-covered garage, high on a hill, sat a new house with a wide expanse of windows overlooking the lake. What a delightful place to live! From that vantage point one could drink in all of God's creation.

As the walkway turned to follow a small inlet, I noticed more ducks feeding in the shallow water. An older man sat on a bench nearby, watching the ducks play "bottoms up" as they worked at the bottom grasses. I thought about sitting on the bench with the man for awhile. But I wasn't halfway around the lake, so I passed on by. Why stop when I wasn't yet tired?

Suddenly I heard a child's squeal and turned to see a toddler running toward the ducks with his mother right behind him. Delight shone in the child's face. The mother pulled a dinner roll from her pocket and broke off small portions. The boy ate one piece of the bread and then threw a piece to the ducks. He walked over to the older gentleman and offered him a piece of roll too. The man smiled, accepted the bread, and laid his hand on the boy's head.

Leaving the inlet, my walk took me past an interesting house set back from the road. A man in a gray flannel bathrobe walked down the driveway and pulled a newspaper from under a shrub. He raised his hand in greeting and called "Good morning!" I returned the greeting with a smile.

As he went inside, I took a closer look at the house. Obviously it had been a railroad depot at one time. Now it was a nice home with well kept shrubs banked around the base of the building. Behind the remodeled depot I recognized the old railroad bed. What sort of stories would the depot tell if it could speak? Would it tell of families who had traveled many hours to spend some time vacationing at this lake? Would it tell of soldiers going off to war?

Would it tell of boys and girls waiting at the depot just to see the big engine? On down the walkway I came across a beautifully kept vegetable garden. The dark ground reminded me of the humus in my father's compost. Above the squash, a scarecrow greeted me, and oblivious of the scarecrow a brown bunny peeked out from under a large leaf. If I hadn't been looking closely, I'd never have seen the small animal. As I approached the other end of the lake I saw "white horses" moving across the lake. Although I knew the horses were nothing but towering columns of steam rising from the warmer waters of the lake, they appeared as horses running with the wind.

The mournful wail of an ambulance echoed from behind me. My thoughts followed the sound. What might the circumstances be? As I walked along I offered a silent prayer for those involved.

Soon I heard the rushing noise of a waterfall, and when the walkway met a narrow one-lane road I turned and followed it across a bridge that spanned a little dam. On the bridge railings lacy spiderwebs, heavy with last night's rain, sparkled in the sunlight like jewels on a queen's robe. The thundering waters below sent a layer of foam down the creek.

Near the end of the bridge I met a jogger coming from the opposite direction, and we both stepped to the side to allow a car to drive across the narrow bridge. Two children, securely buckled into the backseat, waved to me as their mother maneuvered across the narrow bridge. I knew that their school was just down the road and their mother dropped them off on her way to work. I waved back and turned to follow the lakeshore away from the bridge.

As the pathway climbed a little hill I began to wish that I hadn't passed up the opportunity to rest with the man on the bench by the ducks. Now that I needed a break, there was no bench in sight. I found a large rock and leaned against it for awhile.

Beside the rock I pulled aside a long vine of prickly brier, nipping off the tender new shoot and savoring the fresh flavor. The action had been as automatic as brushing a fallen lock of hair from my eyes so that I could see. Below me a flash of orange moved through the water. Another followed it, and soon a whole school of giant goldfish swam in the shallows. Then I remembered the story of how persons who lived around the lake during the summer bought goldfish and then released them when they left at the end of the season. The fish had grown large, many of them a foot or longer in length. Now there were schools of goldfish, some of them bright orange, some black, and some mottled gold and white.

I took the final portion of my walk more slowly as it wandered through a rose garden. There were red roses, yellow roses, white roses, and some of the new hybrid colors. Some blooms were large, as big as a saucer, and some were tiny, clustered with other blooms. Each rose was individual, even those on the same bush. No two roses were exactly alike. The rain had knocked the petals off several of the older blooms, and the morning sun had begun to dry them. I held out the tail of my shirt to form a pocket and scooped up some of the petals. As I left the lake I carried my treasured rose petals carefully.

Laying the petals out to continue drying, I rejoiced in my decision to take the walk with God. I could as easily have decided to roll over and sleep a little longer or to get to my work right away. But I had listened to God's call and made the best choice!

With the refreshment of a shower and the memory of my walk, I turned to face the day. I knew that God and I could deal with anything that came my way!

Chapter 2

SHALL I TAKE THE WALK?

Making Decisions

Maybe I should get up and rush to the many demands of this day. There are never enough hours to accomplish what I set out to do anyway.

How can we simplify our decision process? Decisions sometimes cause us the most problems, and often we labor over the small decisions, thereby complicating our lives even more. Life, by God's creation, is not simple but complex. The psalmist said, "I praise you, for I am fearfully [awesomely] and wonderfully made" (Ps. 139:14 NRSV).

For a moment, imagine that you are handed a gift from God. The gift is beautifully wrapped. You've been told that this is the most wonderful gift of all, but as you sit and look at the gift you hate to disturb the lovely wrapping. You can't imagine that the gift could be more wonderful than the wrapping. But unless you open the gift, you'll never know just how wonderful it is.

In your imagination, lift the gift and feel God's eyes on you as a parent who knows the gift's potential for your happiness and who anticipates your opening it. Now slowly loosen the ribbon. Feel the luxury of the ribbon as it runs through your fingers. Live the anticipation of such a magnificent gift. As you fold back the papers, you realize that the most wonderful gift is actually a personal relationship with God, a one-on-one partnership with the One who created the world, who is ever creating and active in the world.

God's Gift of Joy

Of all creation, God gave humans alone the opportunity to struggle over discovering how we fit into the whole scheme of the universe. Only humans seek joy and the meaning and reason for existence. Sometimes we seek happiness and substitute it for joy.

Happiness happens on the outside.
Joy dwells deep within.
Joy is not a goal but a by-product of service.

- Can true joy come if we strive for more and more and bigger and better "things"?
- Think about a time when you *really* felt joy. You may have to think back a long way.
- Think about what, in that situation, brought you joy.
- Where was your focus?
- How can you transfer that focus into your life today?

There was once a rich young man, as the story goes, who asked what he must do to have true joy. The wise person of whom he asked the question recognized the goals of the young man. The wise person told the young man to go and sell what he had and to reset his goals on God. The young man went away sad, turning down the opportunity for joy because he had much wealth and the wealth was his goal.

This story in Matthew 19:16-24 does not speak against wealth so much as against allowing wealth to rule our lives. If the young man's great wealth had not been the ruler of his life, then he could have felt comfortable in selling what he had in order to follow Jesus.

When we place God's will as our central will, then our lives are simplified. And no matter how complex our schedule becomes, no matter how many pressures we feel, our life becomes easier because we continually look to God for direction. Every decision, every plan, can then be judged according to whether it fits into God's plan for our lives. And that plan is not a blueprint-type plan, but rather a direction that God leads us in every circumstance or encounter.

Knowing God's Will

Most of us today wear many hats.

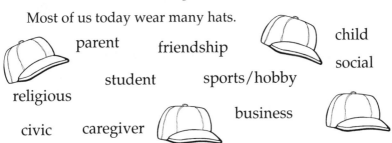

parent   friendship   child
                            social
        student   sports/hobby
religious
                            business
civic   caregiver

How can we balance our many roles and responsibilities of life and still follow God's will?

In Romans 12:2, Paul tells us "Do not be conformed to this world, but be transformed by the renewing of your minds, so that you may discern what is the will of God— what is good and acceptable and perfect" (NRSV). Paul does not suggest that we remove ourselves from the world or lift ourselves above the world. J. B. Phillips's version of Romans 12:2 says, "Don't let the world around you squeeze you into its own mould, but let God re-make you so that your whole attitude of mind is changed. Thus you will prove in practice that the will of God's good, acceptable to him and perfect."

With so many paths to follow, how do I know God's will?

- Does this choice help me to grow in my partnership with God?
- Does this choice turn me away from God?
- Am I claiming this choice as God's will simply to justify what I want to—or what someone else wants me to do?
- Are my actions truly prompted by God—or by what others will say or think about me?

First, we seek God, and then everything else comes into proper order. Nothing should come before God's kingdom, including our desire to simplify our lives. We do not come to the kingdom through simplicity. But when we take the kingdom seriously and work to better God's kingdom, then simplicity comes naturally—the simplicity of focusing on God's call in our lives.

We can, however, become so outwardly simple (in a false way) that we lose our effectiveness. We can also become so hung up on beliefs that we worship the beliefs instead of the true God. We must develop a gospel style of living with more emphasis on lifestyle than on beliefs. The gospel stories tell us how Christ lived and taught, how he demonstrated following God's will instead of concentrating on beliefs and doctrine or on what others (even those of the religious community) thought.

Jesus' life exemplifies a role of living in the world, as he ate with those ridiculed by others and accepted gifts from those who had led questionable lives. Jesus even stood by his disciples when the rulers reprimanded him for allowing them to eat grain from the fields on the Sabbath, which was against the religious rules of the day. Jesus was very much "in" the world, sometimes accommodating to fulfill his goals for God. But he was not "of" the world. Jesus did not compromise his mission for God for the sake of society, even the religious society of his day. God came into the world in Christ.

As we wear our many hats it is well to recognize the talents and gifts that God has given us.

> *My career—that which I do to make a living.*
> *My vocation—my total life as I follow God's calling.*

When I consider my vocation, I recognize ways that I can follow God's will by using God's gifts in all facets of my life. This includes my career, but it also includes my service in and through the church; my dedication to my friends and family and even to those whom I don't know; the way I act in the workplace, in my home, in school, and even in the grocery store. My vocation is a lifestyle. It is using all of God's gifts in a way that follows the divine direction in my life.

What we have is a part of God's kingdom and is a gift from God. Even our talents and intellect are gifts from God. We cannot count our achievements as fruits of our own efforts; rather, we count them as gifts from God. After all, God gave us talents and minds to accomplish achievements.

One of my mother's favorite verses was Philippians 4:13, which tells us that we can do all things through Christ who strengthens us. For years I told myself that I lived by this verse, but one day I realized that I was putting the emphasis on the wrong word. I subconsciously declared that *I* could do all things because I had Christ to strengthen me. It was a sort of exclusive attitude that set me apart from others. Then I realized that the emphasis should be on joy in Christ, joy in how God works through our lives to bring about God's will. The primary word in the verse should be *through.*

God always gives us tools with which to do our calling. The Bible tells us of how God used Noah's carpentry skills, Moses' rod, David's slingshot and harp, the innkeeper's stable, and even the executioner's cross and a borrowed tomb. What tools has God placed in our hands? Think about the gifts that God gave you and how they can be made available and used for others. According to Matthew, Jesus said, "Those who find their life will lose it, and those who lose their life for my sake will find it" (10:39 NRSV). Sometimes we may lose, but didn't Jesus win by losing? To recognize this and work for God's kingdom no matter what, will make a difference in how we live.

Choosing to be Christian does not relinquish our free will. Nothing can take our free will away. God made us that way. Choosing to be Christian is simply choosing to use our free will in the manner that we are directed by God.

As the song says about a beautiful morning: "everything's going my way." This does not mean that everything will be smooth and easy. God did not promise an easy life; God only promised to be with us in that life. But if I choose for my way to be God's way, then everything will be my way, even in hardship. When our choices require suffering, we can realize that God suffers too. It is not God's choice that we suffer. However, when a combination of choices (mine, other people's, and even persons who lived long ago) brings about such suffering, then, as Augustine once put it, "God permits evil, so as to transform it into a greater good."

Choosing God's Way
- Look at God as your vision.
- Seek *first* the kingdom of God.
- Allow God to reshuffle your priorities.

Some Practical Suggestions

In Micah 6:8 we read that God has told us what is good and required of us: to do justice, to love kindness, and to walk humbly with God. Although we are made in God's image, as humans we still need some practical applications to get us started. Here are a few suggestions. As we use them, we must continue to seek to align ourselves with God.

• Keep your eye on the task instead of the results.
• Never make a major decision without allowing a certain number of hours or days for reflection and prayer.
• On a card, list six items or write a sentence of what is most important to you. Carry the card with you and refer to it when making decisions.
• Make decisions ahead of time concerning such things as budgets, gifts to charities, type of job you will seek, social choices you will make, and appropriate use of time.
• Recognize the difference between concern and anxiety.
• See prayer as a process for change in yourself instead of a formula for a product.
• Own your talents and where they can be used, and leave other situations to the talents God has given others.
• Take pride in your call from God. Recognize that *humility*, *humus*, and *human* come from a common root word. In humility we offer ourselves to be used and refashioned by God.
• Make your decision to the best of your ability and then own that decision and move forward instead of wondering if you were right. The time of absolute certainty never comes.

God has made us complex. What a joy that we are complex and not merely puppets. To simplify we must choose to develop the character of God in our own lives. God gave us choice, and we must use that choice to line ourselves up with God's will. Soren Kierkegaard wrote in his book *Purity of Heart Is to Will One Thing,* "I am, therefore I must decide." When I line myself up with God I can decide what to strip away, how to use my time, what to purchase with my money, and just how to live my life.

People, Not Puppets

Dear God,
  Why don't you make it easy on us?
  You could make it so easy by programming us to choose only the right course of action. You could have a lovely world then, you know. Life would run smoothly, and no one would hurt anyone else. How perfect the world would be if you made us love each another.
  But you didn't want that. You wanted to make us like yourself, with a mind of our own. Some people call it a will. You wanted us to decide for ourselves, the way we would act.
  You knew that we wouldn't always choose the right way. You knew it would be hard. But you wanted people, not puppets, so you gave us a will.
  Then you gave us Jesus to follow and the Holy Spirit to help us use your will to create a better world.
  Now, dear God, help me to learn how to follow Jesus' example and to allow the Holy Spirit to work in my life every day.

Amen*

---

* Delia Halverson, "People, Not Puppets," *Accent on Youth!* spring 1981, 21.

Lifestyle Inventory

True	False	
☐	☒	I don't have enough time to myself.
☒	☐	My time with my family and friends isn't adequate.
☐	☒	I often miss my deadlines.
☐	☒	My/our credit card debt gets out of control from time to time.
☒	☐	I don't exercise on a regular basis.
☒	☐	It seems I always want additional clothing.
☒	☐	I purchase items impulsively.
☐	☒	I never seem to have money for giving to mission projects.
☐	☒	I often have trouble getting enough sleep at night.
☒	☐	I wish my life was better balanced.
☐	☒	I have difficulty deciding just what is important in my life.
☐	☒	I find it too bothersome to recycle.
☒	☐	I would like for my family to value togetherness more.
☒	☐	At times I discover that I have nervous habits.
☒	☐	My weight isn't close to what I'd like it to be.
☒	☐	I have no one I feel comfortable sharing with personally.
☒	☐	It seems I forget things more when my life is busy.
☒	☐	Often I catch myself eating food that I know isn't healthy.
☐	☒	My family and friends complain that I'm irritable.
☒	☐	I often wish I were another age.
☐	☒	I often purchase something because of a television advertisement.
☐	☒	My prayers are usually asking and seldom listening.
☐	☒	Worrying about my children spoils my enjoyment of them.
☐	☒	I have not spent a day by myself in the past year.
☐	☒	It is important for me to have things that my friends have.

True	False	
☒	☐	I often lie awake in the middle of the night thinking about my life.
☐	☒	We seldom discuss finances in our family.
☒	☐	Often I attend social events that I do not enjoy.
☐	☒	Many times I feel I cannot reach out to God.
☐	☒	My/our rent/mortgage payment strains the budget.
☐	☒	I often have migraines or tension headaches.
☐	☒	It seems I get every little illness that comes along.
☐	☒	I feel that I should give a larger percentage to the church.
☐	☒	I/we often overdraw the checking account.
☐	☐	I hesitate to talk with others about wanting a simpler lifestyle.
☐	☒	I become restless often, wishing I were somewhere else.
☐	☒	There are many areas of my life I would like to change.
☒	☐	I don't see how my lifestyle affects people I've never met.
☐	☒	Attending worship is not a regular habit in my family.
☒	☐	I hope to accomplish more in a day than is practical.
☐	☒	It's unusual for me to find time to spend privately with God each day.
☒	☐	I use television, reading, sleeping, and so on as an escape.
☒	☐	I procrastinate rather than working on something I find difficult.
☒	☐	I worry about things over which I have no control.
☐	☒	Often I find myself with nothing to do.
☒	☐	Even if I am overcommitted, I have trouble saying no.
☐	☒	I often boast about being too busy.
☐	☒	I seldom meet with people when I have promised to "get together soon."

True   False

☐   ☒   At the end of the month I don't know where the money went.

☒   ☐   I feel that God wants me to do something but I continually resist.

Count the checks in the left-hand column and enter the number here. _____

0-12 You seem satisfied with your lifestyle.

13-25 Most of your lifestyle seems to please you. Share your ideas with others.

26-40 You will want to consider some changes in order to be more satisfied.

41-50 You will be happier with some immediate changes in your lifestyle.

Go back through the list. Put a smile beside items you have worked to change recently. In the left margin rank 1-5 the items you would like to concentrate on immediately.

Chapter 3

STRETCHING
Centering on God

Without stretching exercises, I ran the risk of muscle cramps that would spoil my walk. Proper preparation reaps full benefits.

How many times have we heard the expression, "Don't just stand there, do something!"? Maybe it's time to reverse the phrase. Maybe in today's busy world we should be telling ourselves, "Don't just do something, stand there (in the presence of God)!"

We take so little time to exercise the practice of silence, where we can stretch out to God. Jesus often went away alone. I think of Jesus' time in the wilderness as a period of stretching to God. It happened before he really began his ministry, right after his baptism by John (see Matt. 4:1-11 and Luke 4:1-13). It was a time of stretching and seeking God's direction for his ministry. What a challenge it must have been for him. Just how would he go about this mission set before him by God?

As he looked at his surroundings in the wilderness, Jesus acknowledged his own hunger. There were many persons in the world who also were hungry. It was within his power to turn the stones, which looked very much like loaves of bread, into actual bread and feed himself and anyone else who was hungry. This could satisfy the physical hunger. Surely people would turn to God if they no longer had hungry stomachs. They would also recognize him, Jesus, as the one who fed them! But he knew that such a feast would not satisfy the people's real hunger, and so he rejected that idea, as well as the source of the idea.

In his deliberations over his ministry, Jesus also considered using a dramatic demonstration of power. He could throw himself down from the high point of the temple, right before all of the religious people of the day. God would save him from destruction, and then the world would know that he was a voice from God, and they would be eager to follow him. But Jesus also turned down that opportunity for sensationalism. He rejected this strong temptation for self-acclaim.

And then his temptation came as a compromise, to appease both good and evil. Did it really matter how he went about it as long as he had everyone acknowledging him as Lord? But this too, he rejected. Instead, Jesus chose twelve persons whom he might teach. And those twelve then went into the world, spreading the message to others.

Jesus spent forty days and forty nights in meditation over his career direction. Can't I spend a few minutes each day or a half day a week in meditation with God? Will it make a difference in my life? Will such a disciplined exercise help me to align myself with God and God's direction in my life?

Allow Time to Encounter the Word

It has always amazed me how our ideas can change over the years, and sometimes we can't even pinpoint just when that change took place. As a freshman in college, I was required to take an introduction to the Bible class that required more memorization than study. I particularly hated memorizing the books of the Bible. (Now there's something that hasn't changed. I still can't remember them. I can find them, but don't ask me to recite them!) Later, I had more interesting courses in the Bible, but they were still primarily concerned with memorizing content. In recent years, however, I've had some real encounters with the Bible. In fact, now it has become closer to being *The Word* for me. But I can't tell you exactly when that change came about. I do know that when I kid myself into thinking that I can save time and simplify my life by studying only a specific part of the Bible for some course I'm teaching or some manuscript I'm writing, then I lose the real encounter. I need the time when God speaks to my personal life through the Scriptures.

There are many books on Bible study methods. I've found two methods most helpful to my own study. One is the simple practice of paraphrasing the passage using everyday words and situations from contemporary life. The other method has three parts:

1) I try to put myself in the author's place, visualizing just who the first audience might have been. That usually requires reading the introduction to the particular book of the Bible, found in most study Bibles, and sometimes reading additional helps;
2) then I try to imagine how the passage can be applied to our world today; and
3) finally, I ask what God would like me to gain from the passage.

Because I think more clearly when I write, I use a loose-leaf notebook with three sections in it as I study the Scriptures. One section is for journaling about the day and what's happening in my life. Another section has pages with thoughts on specific subjects or concepts, such as darkness, hope, humility, miracles, talents, and so forth. When thoughts come to me, I jot them down on a subject page or create a new page, noting the applicable scripture. The third section has pages with specific scripture reference headings, arranged in the same order as the Bible. Sometimes I will make a note in one section reminding me to look at a specific place in another section. This notebook, along with any notes I've made in the margins of my "Working Bible," helps me to recall the insights I've received during my study.

No method of Bible study is perfect for everyone. One of the methods suggested here may interest you, or you may want to search out others. You will also find that different styles of study work best for you at different stages in your faith walk. Be flexible, but be consistent in finding some way to center on the Word regularly.

Develop a Plan for Prayer

In an effort to simplify our lives, we sometimes think we can just remove portions of our "busy-ness" and enjoy the void. Instead we often find that the vacant part of our lives becomes filled with something else, and sometimes that something else is even worse than what we removed!

Some years back there was a popular theory called Parkinson's Law put forth in a book by C. Northcote Parkinson. It said that work expands to fill the amount of time allotted for it. Jesus also spoke of this phenomenon in Matthew 12:43-45 when he told of an unclean spirit that, when sent out of a person, wanders and then brings seven other spirits back to the person whose life has been cleaned and set in order.

And so when we sweep our lives clean of certain things, we need to fill them with something better. If we, as Christians, want to simplify our lives, then we must fill that void with time for centering on God. What we fill our lives with can become our master. In fact, even the effort to simplify our lives can become our "Lord."

Setting aside a specific time for prayer and reflection each day requires discipline. Unless we find some way to build it into a routine part of our schedules, it seldom happens. For me, the early morning is usually the best time, before I've begun anything else. Once my mind picks up on the daily schedule, I find it hard to void the world from my thoughts. However, you may find that there is a better time of day for you. It may be when you have completed something routine that you do each day, and then you can easily turn to prayer. Or you may find that you rest better at night if you set time aside just before retiring. Some people benefit from a longer, concentrated time each day, and some find that several short periods work best for them. These times apart might be thought of as "well visits" or times when we visit the well of God for refreshment and life-giving water.

I discovered a very interesting thing about myself some years back when I attended a silent day apart. The format of the day forced me to spend several large blocks of time in silence, drawing on some inspirational writings, but with a lot of dependence on inward listening. I had not realized that I was missing a depth in my prayer life by not having an extended time of study and prayer now and then. I discovered that I needed an occasional extended time with no interruptions. In my shorter times it seemed that I had barely gotten involved in thought or prayer than I had to shift gears and move on to scheduled activities. In fact, often I resented being pulled away from this time with God. I found myself angry over the demands on my time, although many of these were demands that I'd put into place myself. Now I try to use my daily times for short readings and find some extended times each week when I can be more intentional in study and prayer.

We all must work out our own schedules. What is right for me may not be right for someone else. You may find that your prayer life is stimulated when you pray with several other persons. A friend of mine just discovered that several days at a monastery retreat center with no planned schedule brought him closer to God. Some people find help from journaling with Scripture. Some prefer to read and let the written word simply permeate their being without setting anything down on paper.

The important thing is to begin by setting aside some time. Don't begrudge yourself the time, once you've established what suits you best. Know that this time with God actually simplifies your life.

How to Pray?

No one can give you a formula for prayer. Each person must find what suits him or her best. When we don't know how or what to pray, we might take a clue from the child who was saying the alphabet as a prayer. When someone asked about the wisdom of such a prayer, the child said, "It's OK, God can fill in the words."

If you don't have a pattern for your personal time with God, you might try the following two methods and then adapt one to your own needs. Additional thoughts on prayer may be found in chapter 9.

Focus

Ignatius of Loyola created four spiritual exercises for retreat settings. These steps follow his pattern:

1. *Focus on our separation from God and God's magnetic love.* Establish a habit of seeking the loving grace of God and feeling the love bathe us.
2. *Focus on Christ's life.* Seek to be formed in Christ's image, including action, compassion, and discipline.
3. *Focus on the passion and death of Christ.* How can I die or let go of my attachment to the world? How can I simplify?
4. *Focus on the resurrection.* See it as the power to always choose God's way.

Prayer

P *repare yourself.* Find a location that is comfortable and where you will not be disturbed.

R *epeat a simple verse or prayer.* Learn a short Bible verse or prayer or song. Breathe slowly for several seconds, being conscious of your breathing, and then repeat the verse or prayer, or sing the song quietly. You might try 1 Timothy 1:2*b* or a verse from Psalms, perhaps 8:1 or 46:10. Or sing "Spirit of the Living God" or pray Brother Lawrence's prayer, "Lord, make me according to thy heart."

A *ccept God into your heart.* To do this, center into the very heart of you. Concentrate on the part of you that feels love, that feels sadness, the part that is happy when you do for others. Then ask God to come into that part of you.

Y *ield all that bothers you to God.* Whatever is troubling you, turn it over to God. Know that God understands your problems.

E *njoy God's presence.* Just spend some time simply loving God. Then relax in the joy of being loved by God. Feel God's strength and peace.

R *eview how you felt.* I would suggest that you begin a prayer journal, writing down some of the feelings and thoughts that came to you as you prayed. Writing it down makes your feelings and thoughts more concrete.*

---

* Delia Halverson, "Teach Me How to Pray," *Youth!*, February 1990, 20.

Communicate with God Constantly

Over three hundred years ago Nicholas Herman, a monastery cook who was called Brother Lawrence, gave us encouragement in communicating with God at all times and in whatever we do. In his simple way he talked with God while working in the monastery kitchen as well as when he was on his knees in prayer. His classic book, *The Practice of the Presence of God*, tells of his joy in living with God throughout the day, knowing that whether he was showered with blessings or endured trials, his joy came from simply loving and talking to God. His conversation with God was not always vocal, but he continually experienced a consciousness of God.

Frank Laubach, a missionary who developed the "Each One Teach One" method and led prayer retreats across the nation, had a special way to develop a continual consciousness of God. He suggested that we play a "Game of Minutes" by choosing a specific hour of the day and during that time see how many minutes we are conscious of God's presence.

When I began looking for opportunities to share God with children, I found myself much more conscious of God in everything around me. I would look at something and ask myself, "How could I share God with a child in that situation?" Or I might think, "What can I say to a child about God if we were looking at that particular thing together?" Now, even when there is no child in sight I will think, "Thank you, God, for the intricate petals on that flower." I've even been known to look at a decaying stump and suggest to an adult that God uses lichens and mushrooms to recycle the wood. Seeing such things through the eyes of a child has opened up a whole new dimension of God to me. I've learned to pray with my eyes open!

God at Center Stage

James Weldon Johnson wrote a delightful poem about God creating the world. The poem brings out the imagery of God as center stage in all of creation. This is certainly true when we read the story from the Bible. But then what happened after creation? God gave each of us an individual will, and we chose to use our wills for ourselves instead of for God. We humans thought we could do everything ourselves. This foolish idea is represented in Genesis by our eating the forbidden fruit. This is our stubborn statement, "I can do it myself!" Paul gives us a solution to this in Philippians 4:13 when he states that he can do all things *through* Christ.

Like Adam and Eve, we too must recognize our nakedness (or nothingness) without God. We all have our times with the serpent, our times when we believe we can do it ourselves, alone. That's when life becomes a maze of complications. That's when it eventually all falls down around us and we find ourselves in a cycle of buying or achieving status in order to satisfy our desires, only to find that there is another thing or position still ahead that we must buy or achieve. We are caught up in the maze and have difficulty seeing our way out.

God gave Moses a set of ten rules to live by. These rules make a difference in how we live and help us to live together peacefully. However, we would not have needed the rules had we learned, early on, to seek God's direction in everything that we do. We still struggle with following God today, even with the ten laws to guide us. We can't seem to let go of our stubborn statement, "I can do it *myself!*"

If, however, we spend disciplined time with God, listening to God, then our life is simplified because we have only one direction for every facet of life—the direction in which God leads us. No matter how complicated our lives become, when we set our point of reference on God, our goals become simple.

Lookin' and Lovin'

There is a story of a young boy who went to his father's study and stood in the doorway. His father continued to work at his desk until he realized that the boy was there. Then he looked up and asked, "What is it, son? Is there something you need?" The boy only smiled and said, "I don't need anything. I'm just lookin' and lovin'."

When we can come to God, simply lookin' and lovin' and not demanding anything of God, then we have found the simple life!

The first prayers that we teach our children are thank-you prayers. We ask them to list things for which they are thankful. We, too, should regularly express our gratitude to God. Here's an exercise that may help you center on God with a heart filled with love and gratitude.

Why Do We Love?

1. Take out a clean piece of paper and divide it with a line down the middle, from top to bottom.
2. On the left, list as many blessings as you can think of, things for which you feel indebted to God. (Recognize that we are indebted to God for our existence, for all that keeps us alive, and for the community that God created.)
3. Think for a moment about what your life would be like without those blessings.
4. Tear off the left side of your paper (the part with the blessings listed) and crumple that up and throw it away. Imagine that you have none of those blessings.
5. Now concentrate on the blank right side of the paper. Recognize that your love for God should not depend on any of those blessings. Visualize God as the most loving parent that you can imagine, and spend some time standing in the doorway, simply lookin' and lovin'.

Finding Direction

The outside forces on Jesus' life must have brought him a high level of stress. Everywhere he went, people demanded his strength. Crowds pushed against him, the religious authorities constantly tried to trick him, and even his family tried to redirect his ways. If physical simplicity were the answer, Jesus' life certainly qualified. Physically, he lived a very simple life. But that alone could not remove the stress from his life. Jesus knew the secret of pulling away to seek God and to find direction. The Scriptures tell of many times when he went off by himself, simply lookin' and lovin'. From these times apart he gained direction for his life. We too must find our direction by following God's inner bearing as well as by placing constraints on our lives.

On one occasion I was speaking with a man who had left a demanding business position and had moved into a calling in Christian education, which he felt strongly about. Soon after he began his new career, he shared a concern with me. He had spent many hours meeting with volunteers and talking about their role in the church, when he said to himself, "I haven't made a dollar for the company!" When he realized that his responsibility was to make relationships instead of making money he began to find his direction. He later said that it was very freeing to discover his direction.

Of course just finding our direction doesn't keep us free! I've found that the times I'm most frustrated, and often the times I'm not able to sleep well, are times when I may know my direction, but I don't take action. Perhaps I know that I have a deadline and know what is required to meet it, but I resist settling down to work on the manuscript or project. That's when self-discipline comes into play. That's when procrastination is my worst enemy. That's when I need to center on God's direction and then follow that. That's when I need the potter's hand on the outside as well as the inside.

The Bible holds several images of the potter. This was a common vocation in that time, and everyone understood the images. In talking with a potter recently a new thought came to my mind. Suppose a potter worked at the wheel and only used her hands on the outside. What would happen to the pot? It would be impossible to guide the shape. All forces would be pushing inward. So for a potter, it is important to place hands inside too. But if the potter only used his hands on the inside, then there would be no channeling or restraint to give direction. The pot would still lack the form that the potter had in mind. To make a perfect pot, the potter's hands must be on both the inside and the outside of the pot.

Like potter's hands on the clay of the pot, the source of simplicity in our lives must come from the inside and be restrained on the outside. God's direction on the inside gives the guidance, and the physical restraints that we put on our lives help to set the direction of our lives. With an inner guidance, we find it possible to deal with our materialistic desires.

Before my walk around the lake I worked with some stretching exercises. It only makes good sense if I don't want my legs to cramp up during my walk. Each stretch helps me reach a little farther out in my walk!

Chapter 4

DRESSING LIGHT AND COMFORTABLY
Taking Inventory of Material Possessions

*I hurried to the closet to select my cloth-
ing. I needed something light and comfortable, something that fit well but didn't
bind when I walked.*

Dressing for a walk can be as automatic as getting out
of bed, or it may involve extensive deliberation. As we
dress, we sometimes ask ourselves questions about the
weather or the terrain. Or we consciously wonder what
other walkers will think about our clothing. What clothing is in style for such a walk? What will other people
wear? Will I be in the latest fashion? Will I feel out of
place?

On today's walking paths we find every type of clothing imaginable, from simple boxer shorts and tank tops
to expensive walking suits. If it's hot and humid, the
classy walking suit may be too warm. If it's cold we need
layers that can be removed as the body heats up. Do I
overdress for my walk? Does my joy in the walk depend

on how others view me, or does it depend on how I view the world? Just what is the purpose of my walk?

Foundational Garments

The clothing next to the skin fills certain needs. Primarily, it must allow us to function properly during our walk. A proper fitting foundational garment actually allows freedom of movement, just as following God's call allows us freedom to function.

God calls each of us to a vocation—an action of service. In reality, answering that call gives us freedom and simplifies our lives. Once you decide to follow God's call, then all decisions about material things fall into place. God's direction acts as a mirror to check your reflection.

As we saw in chapter 2, your career is what you do to make a living, but your vocation includes all of life, from providing food for your family and hugging your child to building a home for the homeless. God calls us into vocation, and we must align ourselves with God and follow the call in every area of our lives. In order to walk the simple walk, we must take action on God's call.

Any decisions we make must draw us closer to God rather than separate us from God. Sin has been defined as that which separates us from God. Only you can determine your separation from God. Only you can determine whether you love material things or the money that buys material things more than God. Only you can determine whether that love hampers your following what God calls you to do.

John D. Rockefeller was once asked how much money it would take to be satisfied, and he answered, "Just a little bit more!" Money has the ability to become our rival god. Only when we have complete devotion to God can we loosen the grip of money. If we have complete devotion to

God we will have no desire for the accumulation of money or possessions beyond true necessities to carry out what God calls us to do in mission.

Several teachers of simplicity suggest that we learn more about our love for money and material things by writing a money autobiography. These statements may help you think through the relationship between money and your call from God.

A Money Autobiography

- As a child, I saw money as _____

  _____

- My parents grew up with a concept of money that said money is _____

  _____

- Besides my parents, some people or things that influenced my ideas about money as I grew up included _____

  _____

- As I grew up, my feelings toward people in a different financial status than my family were _____

  _____

- In my adult life, my attitude toward money has changed in the following way: _____

  _____

- These persons have influenced the changes in my attitude toward money: _____

  _____

- Now when I spend money for extra items or pleasures I feel _____

  _____

- In order to feel financially secure for the future I_____

  _____

- I would like to change my attitude toward money by

  _____

  _____

Basic Dress

Sometimes our basic clothing for the simple walk involves a change of attitude. Our commercial society has brainwashed us with "necessities" for life. In order to be happy, in order to be successful, in order to be loved, they lead us to believe that we must own anything that they are trying to sell!

Such an attitude even creeps into our speech. When we are hungry, we say that we're *starving*. When a new and better computer hits the market, we say we *need* the computer. We may find that our basic clothing for our walk begins with keeping alert to our attitudes and retraining our speech habits to use the words "want" and "desire" in the place of need.

Do we concern ourselves more in having than in being? Sometimes we love money even more when we don't have any. By changing our attitudes toward acquiring money and the things that money buys, we simplify our lives. The things that money buys are actually gifts from God, for which we act as stewards. But, you may say, I'm the one who studied hard and learned how to make the money that I spend on nice things. In reality, God gave each of us the ability to learn, and so when it comes to the bottom line, God gave the gift of anything we have or anything we earn. As stewards of God's gifts we must use our money and possessions to answer God's call rather than allowing money to use us.

Take a Closet Inventory

At times we cannot even find the basic clothing for our walk because of all the clutter. Every closet needs a periodic cleaning and inventory.

In Exodus, after God delivered the Hebrew people from their oppressors, they grumbled. They had left their food supply in Egypt and were hungry, and so God gave them food. But if they gathered more than one day's supply at a time it spoiled. Gathering only one day's supply indicated trust in God. The hoarding and wasteful consumption of food indicated insecurity. Living a simple life entails trust and recognizing God's guidance.

Scriptures warn us against relying on money and material things that money can buy. Why are we so afraid of taking the scriptural warning to heart? Is it our fear of being without money? Or is it our lack of trust in God? This doesn't mean that we can throw away our money and expect God to care for us, but we must trust and not get hung up on money. With trust we can accept the statements about money in Matthew (6:19; 19:24) and in Luke (6:30-31, 34; 12:15, 33; 16:13).

First Timothy 6:10 (NRSV) tells us "For the love of money is a root of all kinds of evil. . . . " When we love money or the power it brings, then we become blind to others who do not have it and lose all reservations about ways to attain it.

In Peter's day, braided hair and elaborate robes indicated a flaunting elitism of the rich (1 Pet. 3:3). How often do we decide on a more expensive item because it "makes a statement"? How do items in your possession today (house, furnishings, recreational equipment, vehicles, clothing) make a statement? Is the statement for God or for self? What in our society parallels braided hair and elaborate robes? What material signs in our life point to an attitude of superiority? How do we decide what to wear for our walk?

In the early history of our church, as persecution of Christians died out, it became easy to bear the name "Christian." Love of secular materialism spread, even in the church. Some people witnessed against this by withdrawing from "the world" into the desert. They found that they walked closer to God by moving completely away from the material comforts of life. When the world asked "How can I get more?" they asked "What can I do without?" When the world asked "How can I find myself?" they asked "How can I lose myself?" And rather than ask "How can I win friends and influence people?" they asked "How can I love God?" Such a withdrawal from the world helped those early Christians, but it may not be appropriate for us. In reality, we cannot get along in today's world without money. Most of us must learn to live in the world but not of the world.

I cannot tell you what will materially simplify your life. Only you can decide that. And what you decide today may not be applicable next year, or even next month. It is a never ending process, depending on what's happening in your life and in your own spiritual walk with God.

My decisions will be different from yours. For example, because of the type of workshops I often conduct, we need an automobile with ample trunk space. Perhaps you haul around a large number of kids and need a van. Because of my work, our home needs to include space for an office plus a guest bedroom. But your job may require a home with entertainment space for large gatherings.

Up until a few years ago I chose my walking shoes primarily by the price tag. I had no trouble with my feet, and I reasoned that I could buy several very inexpensive shoes for the price of the better built shoe. After I developed heel spurs I learned to appreciate a better built shoe. However, I discovered a compromise by buying a well built shoe, but not an exorbitantly expensive one, and inserting an insole purchased from the drugstore. Now my heel spurs no longer bother me.

To help you determine how to simplify your life materially, try taking this personal inventory.

An Inventory

In order to take inventory for yourself and your family, consider your essential needs in comparison to your wants (those items that would be nice to have).

List requirements for your home/family under headings of "Essential" and "Would be nice."

House (consider items such as an office, entertaining space, privacy because career is so public, added bedroom for another relative, larger washer/dryer, indoor or outdoor play area, and so on)

Essential   Would be nice

Clothing

Essential   Would be nice

Entertainment

Essential   Would be nice

Automobile/transportation

Essential   Would be nice

Paid Services

Essential   Would be nice

Look over your list. Are there some items you have placed under the "essential" column that could be moved into the other column if you changed your lifestyle?

Wise Purchases

There comes a time in every walker's life when new clothing must be purchased. In order to keep your closet inventory simple, consider these questions before making a purchase.

- Must I own this, or is there a way to enjoy it without owning it?
- Do I own something else that will serve the same purpose, or is this simply a gadget that I must store between infrequent uses?
- Can I recycle something that I already own rather than purchasing new?
- Is it more economical to purchase this item in large quantities, or will it spoil before it is used? How can I store it to reduce spoilage?
- If this is a timesaving item, how will the time saved enable me to follow God's call?
- Is this purchase contributing to an addiction? (Even certain foods, clothing, or collectibles can become addictions.)
- Can the packaging of the item be recycled or can it be purchased without packaging in order to reduce our mammoth garbage problem?
- Can I live without this item and give the purchase price to God's work in some way? (Each time I think "I wish I had _____" I will remember that the money went for God's work.)
- Can I purchase one of these items for myself and one to be given to someone else who needs it?
- Have I allowed sufficient thinking time before this purchase, or am I operating under impulse?
- What research went into my decision for this purchase? (Time for research is well spent if you don't have to sit around waiting for someone to come and repair the item later, thereby complicating your schedule.)

- Does this item contribute to the betterment of humankind and the environment? Of what is it made? Under what working conditions do the manufacturers operate?
- What is the real reason for this purchase? Is it to "make a statement" of my material worth?
- How will this purchase help me to follow God's call to vocation?

Choices

A quote from George MacDonald in *A Guide to Prayer for All God's People* suggests, "To have what we want is riches, but to be able to do without is power" (p. 248). The power that comes from choosing to do without is called freedom. If our primary concern is not to make money but rather to follow God's calling, then we are detached from the "world" and free.

Detachment frees us from the control of others. No longer can we be manipulated by people who hold our livelihoods in their hands. Things do not entice our imaginations, people do not dominate our destinies.*

The more we have, the harder it is to make stewardship choices. Voluntary poverty is clean cut. The choice is made for poverty, and we no longer worry. Persons like Mother Teresa have made such choices. However, everyone in poverty does not live a simple life. Sometimes persons in poverty worship money as much as someone who has ample money and still wants more. Whatever our situation in life, in order to have true simplicity in life we must answer God's call in every decision we make.

* Richard J. Foster, *Freedom of Simplicity* (New York: HarperCollins, 1981), 57.

As clothing can encumber or enhance a walk around the lake, so our choices about our material possessions can encumber or enhance our spiritual walk with God. Yet, in the same manner, just buying the proper clothing and putting it on does not result in the walk. Once we've chosen our clothing and are dressed for the walk, we must take that first step forward.

Chapter 5

STEPPING OUT
Evaluating Time Schedules

*All parts of my body were working
together, and they moved with a purpose.*

As I stepped out on my walk, I found myself trying to
push for a faster pace. Then I remembered that pushing to
walk faster brought me frustration rather than help in covering the ground faster. And so I consciously made myself
reach ahead farther with each step. My pace began to
increase, and I no longer felt like a windmill. By reaching
ahead with my feet, the other parts of my body seemed to
fall into place, and they moved with a purpose.

Where in my scheduling of time each day can I reach
out and pull myself together with a purpose? Just what is
happening in the time frame of my life?

Self-Discipline

I lived in Key West, Florida, when I was a senior in high
school. Key West is typically the end of the road for someone who wants to get away from the cold of winter! On
one Christmas Day, when my pastor father closed the

church building for the night, he discovered a young man kneeling by the literature table and translating the Bible into the language of an African people where his parents had been missionaries. His name was Roy, and he had no place to spend the night. My parents quite naturally took him under their wing. But housing was scarce in Key West, and we already had two families living in the parsonage with us. So Dad found some wide boards, and he and Roy laid out a flooring in the attic of our little garage. The roof was so low that Roy had to stoop over in order to walk around, but the place became home for the young man for several months. It kept him out of the few rainy days we had that winter, and he found enough odd jobs to earn him a few dollars while he worked on his Bible translation.

We teenagers thought Roy quite strange. One of the most unusual things about him was the way he budgeted his time. He felt that time was a gift from God, and he kept a log of what he did during the twenty-four hours of each day using five minute increments. Perhaps Roy took his schedule-keeping a little too far, but now that I look back I recognize that self-discipline of time helps us to actually simplify our lives. We need to work toward the right schedule, not in order to squeeze more activities into our days, but in order to achieve a balance for our lives.

A few years ago I took a full-time staff position that was new for that particular church. After about a year, there was some concern on the part of some members of the governing board that the job actually did not warrant a full-time employee. In order to justify the money spent on my salary I was asked to keep a record of the time I spent on phone calls, visits, counseling with teachers, meetings, preparation for events, and all the other activities that filled my days. To my surprise I found that the assignment actually helped me as much as it helped the church council. Sometimes in the frustration of a busy schedule I came away feeling like I was only spinning my wheels. But as I looked at the way I spent my time I did recognize purpose in all of the nitty-gritty things that took up my day. I realized that I was accomplishing my goals and not just spinning my wheels. There were a few places that I found I could adjust my schedule to make me more productive, but for the most part it simply gave me a good understanding and a more simplified direction for my busy day. Seeing it in simple black and white affirmed my mission.

Just like a budget helps you to regulate your spending, a serious survey of your time will help you discipline yourself. In 1 Peter 1:13-16 we are encouraged to discipline ourselves and become "holy."

Just what does the word "holy" mean, and how does it relate to being disciplined? Holy may be defined as something set aside.

God, give me the discipline to recognize that you set me aside in a special way, and that my response to that specialness is to follow your call. And help me to see that following your call requires discipline—discipline of my time. Amen.

All of my life I've enjoyed absorbing myself in a good novel. When I was a junior in high school I came to an understanding about myself that I must deal with continually. Suddenly one day I realized that when I get involved in reading a novel I don't want to put it down. Every time my mother reminded me of some obligation I had or if my sister interrupted my reading to ask me a question, I became very irritable. In fact, I must have been miserable to live with once I started a good book.

I believe that I actually enjoyed living the lives of those

characters in the story. Perhaps I felt that my own life was not exciting enough, and so I used the novels as an escape, much the way that some people use drugs. Finally I decided to give up living other people's lives through the novels and began concentrating on developing an exciting life of my own. I can remember actually making that decision one day and then deliberately going about creating excitement in my own life. After some years away from novels, I went back to reading them from time to time. But it does require a great amount of self-discipline on my part. Even as I write this book I struggle with the call of a good novel that I want to read. I have to create a sense of pride in leaving the novel on the table when I have other obligations—pride in sticking to a schedule or plan.

Now and again I find myself waking in the middle of the night and unable to go back to sleep. Sometimes this happens because of something I've had to eat or drink, particularly late at night. But when this happens frequently, and it doesn't seem to be connected to my diet, then I know that I'm falling down on my self-discipline. I realize that I'm giving in to my old enemy of procrastination. There is usually some manuscript, some workshop preparation, or some household job that I'm putting off. Once I check my schedule and discipline myself, the wakefulness goes away. It's amazing how it can become a vicious cycle. The more I give in to procrastination, the less sleep I get, and the less alert I am to do my work during the day. Then that causes me to procrastinate more, convincing myself it's because "I didn't get enough sleep." But once I break that cycle and get to the core of my problem, I sleep better and become more productive during the day. If sleep is a gift from God, then perhaps God uses that sleep (or lack of sleep) to help nudge me back into the proper use of my time.

I firmly believe that we are made with a need to reach

out to God. I also believe that God constantly reaches out to us. When I don't allow God to reach me during the daytime, my sleep is interrupted at night. God must care a lot to be so persistent.

Evaluate Your Activities

Use the form below to help you recognize just how you spend your time. Is there a good balance? How could it be adjusted?

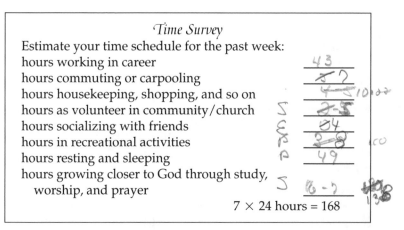

Time Survey
Estimate your time schedule for the past week:
hours working in career
hours commuting or carpooling
hours housekeeping, shopping, and so on
hours as volunteer in community/church
hours socializing with friends
hours in recreational activities
hours resting and sleeping
hours growing closer to God through study,
    worship, and prayer
                                    7 × 24 hours = 168

Now take a few minutes to list all of the specific activities you have taken part in during the past week. Include such items as taking children to sports events, shopping for groceries, writing letters to relatives, commuting, and so forth.

Carefully scrutinize the activities and place the following letters beside each according to whether they are essential to:

P   physical health of yourself and/or your family.
E   emotional/intellectual health of yourself and/or your family.
S   spiritual health of yourself and/or your family.

Look over your list. If your time is void in one area, then you may need to search out ways to grow in that area. Review the direction that you see God calling you. That calling may require a heavier emphasis on one area, but it should not rule out the other two. Recognize that all three of these areas are important. We are told that Jesus grew in wisdom, in stature, and in favor with God and people. Jesus grew in physical, emotional/intellectual, and spiritual health.

Overcrowded Schedules

It has been said that haste is the sin of Adam. He wanted to know of the fruit right *then*. Adam wanted *instant* knowledge.

My father had a favorite saying that I must recall for myself from time to time. He would often remind me, "Little folks want what they want right now, but big folks can afford to wait." Haste often leads to overcrowded schedules.

One day recently I took a serious look at my day's schedule. I had two meetings, a volunteer afternoon at the hospital, and an item to research at the library. Suddenly I became frustrated, just wishing that the day were over and behind me. Then I thought about each item. The meetings were actually times for planning things that I wanted to do, both of which I had a good deal of excitement over. If either of the meetings had been the only thing I was doing that day, I would have looked forward to it with anticipation, savoring every minute of preparation for it. The same was true about the volunteer and research times. Instead, I was wishing my life away by dreading the frustration of my schedule.

One of my greatest sins is a tendency to boast about my busyness. I call this a sin because such boasting does not point out God's use of me as a tool, but rather puts the emphasis on myself. It separates me from God's direction for my life. Perhaps this is a throwback to the idea that we aren't serving God unless we are busy.

When we boast about our busyness or allow others to boast of it for us, we only remove ourselves from the God-centered goal. We accept this busyness as our own doings instead of God's work through us.

In my youth the Martha and Mary story bothered me. It seemed that Martha was concerned about Jesus and his needs, but Jesus was putting Martha down because of her concern. As I've tried to come to grips with my own busyness I realize that Jesus did appreciate other people's concern for him. In fact, the primary focus of his ministry was toward helping others and allowing himself to be served by others. He accepted and affirmed the woman who tended to his tired feet (Luke 7:36-50). He saw that the hungry multitude ate, and he later said, "Truly I tell you, just as you did it to one of the least of these who are members of my family, you did it to me" (Matt. 25:40 NRSV).

In the story about Martha and Mary, the problem was not the jobs that Martha held so important, but rather the fact that she was distracted by her jobs when there was a better choice at the time. Martha was looking for praise for her busyness when she should have grasped the moment and enjoyed basking in the love and teachings of Jesus.

Why do we continue to make our world such a rushed world? When we rush we cannot center our souls and reach inward. Perhaps, even amidst our busy schedules, we should find some way to center our souls and reach inward to God. Amos told us, "Do two walk together unless they have made an appointment?" (Amos 3:3 NRSV). That appointment may not always be for a long period of time. It may be only a passing moment to center on God.

Ready for God's Involvement

Read the story Jesus told in Luke 12:35-40.

Reflect on these thoughts:

- Usually we cite this passage when we talk about the second coming of Christ. Might it have a more immediate meaning in your life?
- Might this mean being ready to receive God's personal involvement in your life *every* day and at *any* hour?
- How can you live on the edge, as if you expect God to become personal to you in any act of the day? What sort of surprising joy will this bring?
- Try reflecting on specific events from this week with the questions, "How did God work through me in that particular thing I did?" or "How can I see God in that situation?"

Prioritizing Time

There have been occasions in my life when I suddenly realized that I could simplify my life by adjusting the way I spent my time, by prioritizing my time. Some of these realizations came as a jolt out of the blue, some were gift ideas from other people, and some came to me as a gradual awareness. Perhaps my sharing these with you will help you to prioritize your time.

- *I don't have to blow-dry my hair!* What a relief to put the dryer in the guest bath and not have to deal with it every morning.
- *I can turn off the television or move into another room!* Rather than watching a program just because I plan to watch the one during the next hour, I can be choosy. By turning off the TV in between programs or moving into another room, I've discovered that I enjoy my choice of programs even more.
- *I don't have to finish a book!* This one came on me suddenly. I think it was a hangover from my book report days

at school when I would labor through a book just to make a report. I experienced joy in the deliberate decision to return a book to the library unfinished because I really found that it was not something that I wanted to read.

- *I need only read enough of a newspaper article to get what I want from it.* Perhaps my course in newspaper article writing taught me this. We were instructed to give all information concerning who, what, when, and where in the first few sentences. Now, once I determine these things I decide whether it's important enough for me to continue reading the rest of the article.

- *I can throw a piece of junk mail away without even opening it.* We become bombarded through the mail with demands for our time and money. Periodically I request that my name be taken off mailing lists by writing to Direct Marketing Association, 6 East 43rd St., New York, NY 10017.

- *Regular maintenance and storage of equipment saves time.* When I maintain my equipment (and my body too!), it's ready when I need it and I cut down on last minute stress. Proper maintenance also gives the equipment a longer life and reduces shopping time for new items (or time at a doctor's office to repair my body).

- *Complaining about something is a waste of my time unless I plan to do something about it myself.* This is where the Thirteenth Generation (or Generation X) has the right idea. We older generations tend to spend a lot of time deliberating about something without getting down to action. This translates into complaining with no intention of taking any action ourselves. The younger generation says, "If something needs to be done, let's get busy doing it and talk about it as we carry out the action."

It takes a conscious effort on my part to tell myself that my time is too precious to spend complaining or debating an issue unless I will personally take the time to do something about my complaints. This saves me many an hour of debate over whether our city or national officials are carrying out their duties or whether a committee in the church is functioning properly.

My mother's father used to tell her, "Edith, make yourself useful as well as ornamental." We might also say, "Put your action where your words are."

• *Leisure is an attitude rather than an activity.* Sometimes the leisure time activities that I plan only leave me drained and frustrated, particularly when my mind is on things I have left undone. Today people tell us to be kind to ourselves and give ourselves recreation and relaxation time. But unless I adjust my attitude and truly leave my other responsibilities behind, I return from the R & R time more frustrated than before it began. This time becomes an obligation to "be kind to myself." I often have a truer feeling of leisure as I complete a task and bask in the completion of it than if I put it off in order to do some recreational activity.

During the week after Christmas a friend from a small town said, "We celebrate Christmas all week around here. Most of us take vacation days after Christmas, and then we visit in each other's homes and relax without the stress of preparation."

There must be a balance, and we must prepare ourselves for work and play.

Determine Your Work Style

A friend of mine said that her problem is that she's both a morning and an evening person! If she's to be most effective, this leaves her the middle of the day and the wee hours of the morning to sleep. I've learned that occasionally when I am on a roll I can be productive late into the night, but usually my most effective time for writing or planning comes in the morning.

My husband works best when he accomplishes one thing before he moves on to another. I'm more prone to bounce from one thing to another, letting one item mull in the back of my mind while I work on something else. I do find, however, that I must watch myself so as not to become distracted when I have deadlines to meet. A friend discovered that deadlines cause her undue stress. She decided not to accept any assignments that require deadlines. Fortunately, her job does not require deadlines. We may not have that freedom, but there is something else we can do. If we can set our own deadlines, we can build in a cushion of time between our personal deadlines and those required by others.

Complete this checklist to determine your work style.

'What's My Work Style?

I work best ___ in the morning ___ in the evening.

I like to ___ get a whole job finished at once ___ do a little of a job each day.

I function best by laying out plans ___ a day at a time ___ a week in advance.

I prefer ___ a routine schedule each day ___ a varied schedule.

I function best ___ by working on an idea while the creative thoughts are coming and refining it later ___ by refining as I go along.

I concentrate best ___ in utter quiet ___ with background music or noise.

I am most creative ___ after having something to eat ___ when I'm hungry.

I can work ___ when my physical surroundings are in order ___ in confused surroundings.

I find that deadlines ___ move me to action ___ cause me severe stress.

I like to have ___ all information about a project on one
page ___ miscellaneous notes about the project that I can
shuffle into an order.
My concentration time usually lasts for about _____
minutes without a break.

Making Life Events Meaningful

Sometimes our frustration over our schedules comes
more from feeling that we don't have time for the exciting
life that other people seem to lead. We begin to think that
we lead a dull life. There is a difference between a quiet
life and a dull life. A dull life has no purpose or spark. A
dull life plods along (or even scurries around) without a
goal.

But a quiet life has an attitude of peace within self. A
quiet life sees reason and goals in everything that happens. A quiet life can be a very busy life or it can be limit-
ed in events. A quiet life centers in on God and can find
God in everyday events.

In the July/August 1994, issue of the devotional magazine *alive now!* Jean M. Blomquist shared how eating a
simple meal has become holy. She questions, "What if, as I
filled my body with food, I also filled my mind and heart
with the fullness of Christ—the power, compassion, healing, forgiveness, affirmation of life that he lived each
day?" (p. 43). She reminds us that each meal gives us new
life, a new dependence on God and on the earth, and a
reminder that Christ said, "Do this in remembrance of me;
do this as oft as ye drink. . . . "

Our days are filled with alternative joys, opportunities
to experience joy without expense or extra time. With
them our lives can be exciting in a quiet way.

We humans divide life into little categories, and we
frantically go about trying to balance all of the categories.
However, God sees life as a whole. That's why Jesus was

Alternative Joys

! Listening to and identifying nature sounds.
! Learning identification of all trees on routine routes of travel.
! Observing different color tones and recognizing that God could have made everything in black and white.
! Identifying bird songs.
! Observing different textures and marveling in them.
! Discussing and reflecting on happy occasions during the week.
! Looking in the eyes of those to whom we speak and thanking God for them.
! Thanking God for the gift of taste as we eat.
! Marveling over the way that God created our bodies, such as making our noses in such a way that the shower water doesn't drown us.
! Recognizing that God could have made us to require no sleep, and so sleep is a gift from God.
! Looking for the dependability of God in nature, including sunset and sunrise, tides, movement of stars, seasons, and cause and effect of our actions.
! Appreciating God's love as shown through other people.
! Experiencing a Sabbath with each change of activity.

---

able to see the potential in the rough fisherman called Simon, a potential of a solid foundation for the church.

What would it be like to have God look into our eyes, deep into the soul? First there would be a fear of recognition of our pettiness, of our busyness with no direction. Then there would be a joy of acceptance, even in our pettiness and busyness. This would be followed by a desire and dedication to change and to follow God's desire for our lives.

Giving our time and our schedules to God is a form of stepping out and reaching ahead instead of pushing to go faster. In doing this, all parts of the body will work together, and move with a purpose.

Chapter 6

LISTENING ALONG THE WAY

Staying Alert to Others

How had I missed these sounds earlier? I had been so bound up in my own thoughts that I missed all that was happening around me!

Everywhere we turn in today's world we find noises. Some noises are pleasant to the ear and some create stress. As I walked around the lake there were many nature noises as well as noises of civilization. I had to listen attentively to sort them out. There were songbirds, ducks and geese, wind through the trees, a sudden splash as a fish jumped, and the roar of the waterfall. There was the regular footfall of the runner's shoe on the wooden bridge, children's voices as they pedaled bikes to school, and car tires crunching rocks in the road. Even the distant wail of the ambulance siren blended with other sounds, unless I deliberately listened.

Several years ago I took a walk along another lake. As I walked, I had my ear tuned to the sounds of many songbirds declaring their praise to God. Suddenly a flock of grackles swooped over the ridge and silenced the songbirds. As their chatter took up all the sound waves, I scowled at them and scolded them for distracting me from my own praise prayer. Then a thought came to my mind. Perhaps it was God's presence nudging me to thought, just as Jesus had to scold the disciples for turning the children away. I thought, "That outrageous chatter is the only voice that God gave those grackles. How else can they praise God but by an incessant chatter?"

Since then when I hear blackbirds I remember a line in the hymn "Morning Has Broken" that speaks of blackbirds singing praise.

A year ago I moved into a delightful neighborhood next to a neighbor who enjoys birds. Her love for birds is all-inclusive. Each morning she throws pieces of bread out on her lawn for the blackbirds. Each day she also fills many tiny feeders with birdseed for the songbirds.

I'm reminded to listen to each person's voice, to each of God's creatures raising prayer to God; some praising and some asking; some crying in frustration and some shouting resentment. If God calls us to minister to others, how can our listening act as a tool for God to minister to these voices?

Why Listen?

There is a definite difference between hearing and listening. When we hear something we are in a passive mode. In order to listen we must become active.

It's like the five-year-old who doesn't respond to the teacher until spoken to five times. When asked why there was no response the first time spoken to, the child answers, "When my mother means something she says it five times." That kid hears in order to count the number of times, or in order to recognize the tone of voice that signals the end of patience, but the child is not actually listening until that fifth time.

It makes us wonder if the voice is even there when there

is no one listening. It's like the age-old debate. When there are no eardrums to pick up the sound and relay it to the brain, is it truly sound or is it simply some electronic waves? Something to think about. By listening we use the tools God gave us.

Sounds
I saw a leaf fall
to the ground,
It only made the
slightest sound.
I didn't see the
next one fall.
And so it made
no sound at all.
—Sam Halverson

Active listening not only helps us to become aware of what the person is saying but encourages persons to continue the thought process, to continue sharing. By listening actively we act as God's tools. We place ourselves in alignment with God in a sort of intercessory prayer mode. We are actively involved where God wants us. Perhaps we might call it being "on the listening edge."

On the Listening Edge
- Be sensitive to feelings as well as words.
- Watch for body language.
- Recognize meanings in different tones of voice.
- Maintain good eye contact. Let your eyes do some talking!
- When appropriate, give an occasional hug or touch on the arm.
- Affirm your interest with an occasional nod, a smile, or a brief word or two.
- Resist forming answers as you listen. That comes later if required.

- Recognize that an answer or advice is not always appropriate.
- Analyze your answers. Do your words encourage conversation or thought, or do they act to control, manage, or convince others to your own belief?
- Appreciate silence in a conversation. Sometimes it's during those silent interludes that God breaks through.

Because our world's so filled with sound, we often think of silence in a negative way. Some people do their thinking while they talk, and others must think before they speak. In either case, we should allow silence to happen in a conversation.

Try an experiment this week. During lulls in conversations, instead of talking, try listening and see how much you can learn about the other person. How does it feel? The more you practice, the more comfortable it should become. When you're tempted to speak up, say to yourself, "I can use silence as active listening."

Must I Agree?

Listening to someone does not necessarily mean that we agree with the person. Often we are confronted with decisions on a particular issue. We struggle with the pros and cons and feel unsure about our final decision.

When pressed to make a decision on an issue, in the heat of excitement, we find ourselves losing the ability to think clearly, and our decision making often becomes only an emotional response.

Deciding on an Issue
1) *Realize that you don't have to hold an opinion on everything.* If you are not well versed enough on a subject, leave the decision to those who are well versed. History shows

that poor decisions are made by people ill prepared to make such decisions. However, we need to realize that sometimes not taking a stand for something is a decision in itself—a decision against the situation. If you are not well versed on the subject, then postpone your decision until you can learn the facts.

2) *With a cool head, look at both sides of the issue.* This is where the listening comes into play. Ask opinions of people, and ask them *why* they hold such opinions. The why is more important than just the mere fact that an influential person holds that opinion. If the person doesn't know why, then he or she isn't well versed on making the decision either.

3) *Learn the qualifications of the decision.* What is required in such a situation? If you are not knowledgeable about the requirements, become educated. Go to an outside source to find the requirements. Seek information from someone not tied up in the emotions of this particular issue.

4) *Make your decision for yourself.* Now, look at the situation and determine for yourself whether the qualifications are being met. It was once said that "a man who trims himself to suit everybody soon whittles himself away." Recognize the importance of you, of being your own person and being entitled to your own stand on an issue.

5) *Stand behind your decision.* Once you have made your decision, stand by that decision all the way. It takes real courage to stand up for your convictions, but you can do it after you go through a sound process in making that decision.

Listening in Order to Know

As we engage in active listening, it is important to remember that each person is unique and each of us is at a different stage in our spiritual journey. Sometimes we complicate our lives by assuming something about a person. In Matthew 7:6 Jesus tells us not to cast pearls to swine because the swine don't appreciate them. They will trample them underfoot and turn and maul you. Paul picks up on this same theme in Hebrews 5:11-14 when he refers to feeding milk or meat.

By listening, we recognize that some folks are not ready to receive certain ideas or suggestions that we may want to offer. It becomes a waste of time and can also threaten our relationships with persons if we feed them pearls when they can't appreciate them.

Standing in Another's Shoes

Poor relationships cause stress, thereby complicating our lives. We can simplify our relationships and therefore our lives by standing in another person's shoes. This form of listening helps us to view the situation from that person's perspective.

As I listened to the toddler's squeals of delight over the ducks, I tried to recall recent times when something excited me so much that joy simply burst from within. By stepping into the toddler's shoes, I enriched my life.

When I heard the sound of the ambulance rushing down the distant highway, I thought of someone aching with pain. Emotionally stepping into that person's shoes helped me to form a prayer for healing, even though I had no knowledge of who the person might be.

Jesus told the story of the Samaritan who went beyond what was even expected of him. It might have been expected for him to tell the authorities at the next town about the dying man. But the Samaritan recognized what it would be like to have been beaten and left for dead. If this story were set today, the Samaritan wouldn't shy away, wondering if the man has AIDS. He would place the man in his own car, drive him to the nearest hospital, probably several miles off the interstate, pay for the emergency room treatment, and sign a credit sheet for his own charge card, saying, "If there's anything else that this man needs to get him back on his feet, just put it on my credit." An open-ended credit—that's the ultimate experience of standing in another person's shoes.

John Wesley suggested that we not set a time for expecting Jesus to return, but that we expect him at any moment. Indeed Jesus is returning any moment, in our children, in our spouse, in our friends, and in the homeless person on the street. Dare we step into Jesus' shoes to understand what he's going through?

Try This!

1) For one day, pray for those you meet that day.
2) As you meet each person, mentally say a prayer for that person. Concentrate on something you know about that person. You might lift up a problem the person has, or you might simply think about what he or she is wearing.
3) Take an inventory at the end of the day and determine the percentage of time you remembered to pray.
4) Try this every day for the rest of the week.
5) What percentage of time each day were you able to remember to pray for persons?

YOU ARE ON YOUR WAY TO A HABIT!
Remember, it takes six weeks to form a habit. You only have five more to go.

Listening Develops Friendship

As a true product of today's mobile society, I've moved more than twenty times in my life. Each move brings new friends, and inevitably someone feels it a bounden duty to tell me the unpleasant things about another person I am about to meet.

Each person brings to a friendship or relationship his or

her own personality. We see each new relationship through glasses colored with our own background. Something unpleasant to one person may not hold true for another. In fact, I usually find myself leaning in the opposite direction. Once I've been told something adverse about that person, I make a determined effort to find something good.

For years I felt guilty when I did not spend equal time with all of my friends. Then I realized that there are different levels of friendship. Somewhere in the past I heard a definition that divided friendship into three distinct categories: intimate, close, and casual.

Intimate friends are few and far between. There may be only two or three friends in your lifetime that you could actually call intimate. It's also possible that your personality doesn't allow intimate friends. The more intimate the friend, the less necessity there is for talking. A common feeling and understanding flows, with no need to express it. Intimate friends can reveal things to each other that would kill any other type of friendship.

Close friends are more prevalent. Yet the relationship offers great rewards. Close friends enjoy many things in common. They thrive on the give and take of conversations of mutual interests. They share their excitement and joys, as well as their sorrows. A close friend may develop into an intimate friend, given the right environment. Listening without assuming helps to deepen friendships here.

Casual friends are many. They develop with neighborhood locations, business associates, and through other friends. They are the wildflower garden of life. Growth depends on the location and climate.

Use your own judgment to determine friendships. Don't assume anything only by what someone else tells you, but listen with an open ear. Listening helps us learn about another person and brings a friendship into play.

A part of the excitement of a new friendship is discovering the common kindlings that spark that relationship. When we stifle this search for common interests, we lose a part of the motivation to develop the friendship.

We can simplify our lives by recognizing that everyone we meet may not become a friend and that some friendships warrant more time than others. Jesus did teach us to love everyone, but that doesn't mean that we must spend the time developing intimate or even close friendships with everyone.

Giving Self, a Freeing Experience

The Greek language uses four words for love.

Storge—affection, similar to the love of a parent for child, spouse for spouse.

Philia—love for friends, or friendship. The name for the city of Philadelphia comes from this word.

Eros—a sexual love in which the person loved is desired as an object.

Agape—love that requires nothing in return, an outgiving freeing love.

In our world today, we use the word "love" in many ways. We *love* pizza. We *love* to go to the beach. We *love* our job or our home. We *love* our spouse, or our boyfriend or girlfriend, or our children or teacher. And we also *love* God. But yet inwardly we know that we do not have the same emotion for each of these. And when we read Jesus' command for us to love one another and to love our enemies, we have difficulty shuffling through just what emotion we should cultivate for whom, just how we should love our enemies.

Agape (pronounced: ah GAH pay) might be called an "other oriented" love. This love gives self to others. Through this love we step into others' shoes and recognize love from that viewpoint. Through this love we accept others for who they are. Through this love we begin to enter into the heart of God, to allow God to use us as a tool to channel love. We no longer have to worry about evaluating a person, but we accept as God accepts. *Agape* becomes a freeing experience of giving to others. In this freeing experience we channel our love only in the way that God would have us go.

Perhaps one of the reasons we fill our lives with noises and avoid listening is that we fear being purposeless. We feel that if we fill our lives to the brim, at least some of it will have a real purpose. In *agape* we don't just give ourselves without a purpose. We give with the purpose of channeling God's love. Giving self with this purpose doesn't deplete, but rather refills. It is like a bucket that miraculously refills as fast as we can dip out of it. But if we don't dip out, then evaporation takes its toll and the bucket dries up.

This love for others that God desires for us is not something that always comes naturally. In fact, we often must force ourselves to reach out to others in love even when we have difficulty putting our hearts into it. Then suddenly, when we see the reaction of the person who has benefited from our actions, it reaches into us and becomes our love. That's when love for others, when *agape*, changes us.

Chapter 7

OBSERVATIONS ALONG THE WAY

Seeing God in the Ordinary

My walk took me between the lake and a road. So many things to observe! Like my life, the world is filled to the brim with signs of God.

My father taught me to watch for the unusual and to appreciate it in many ways. Both of my parents taught me to appreciate folks, to look at them and find something good in them that I could treasure. However, where Mother's focus was on accomplishing what she set out to do, Dad taught me to watch for God's little surprises along the way and to wonder about the people I meet. He was an amazingly sensitive man for his era.

When we watch for God in the people and things we encounter every day, we awaken our consciousness to God throughout the day. We become more at one with the universe God created and therefore closer to God. We place ourselves "in the shoes" of another person and begin to see that person in the way God sees him or her. We move from a self-centered world to a God-focused world. These might be called spontaneous experiences with God.

Most of this chapter gives examples of my own reflections that have drawn me closer to God. Perhaps these examples will give you some idea of how simple these spontaneous experiences with God can be.

Removing the Clutter

As I remember the vine-covered garage along the lake I think how much it is like our lives. Undeniably each person who sees that garage forms different thoughts. To some, it's just a tangled mass of vines. Some folks will think, "What an eyesore. Why don't they tear it down?" Another person may wonder just what is inside and when it was last used.

My mind went back to when the garage was first built. I could visualize the owner's pride. I'm sure the garage was adequate for the family car. How like our lives: what's adequate today becomes inadequate later, whether physical items, lifestyles, or attitudes. But do we continue to hold on to them, trying to fit a too large automobile into a too small garage? And when we finally realize that it no longer fits, how do we change? Do we ignore the inadequacy? Do we enlarge and expand our vision? Do we view it from another perspective? Or do we tear it down and completely rebuild? Reflecting on God's direction simplifies such decisions.

New Uses for the Old

The depot-turned-house that I saw on my walk had been given a new direction. For years we Americans felt that everything must be new. The old was set aside to make room for the new!

I recall one year when my husband, Sam, and I thought we would retire our living room furniture and buy all new items. Living in a very small town, we made a special trip to a furniture store in a larger community. The salesman proudly showed us from room to room, explaining how he had selected the furnishings and coordinated the rooms. He tried to convince us to purchase a room complete. A large sign in each room stated the price of the room if purchased item by item. It also quoted the reduced price of the room complete, down to the last lamp and letter opener.

If we filled our living room with all of the items he had selected, there would be no space left for the personal things we had at home. In some people's eyes, the simple thing to do would have been to throw away all of the miscellaneous items we'd accumulated throughout the years and bring in a whole new room. Why waste time making such decisions? Why not let the salesman spend the time for you?

This might simplify the time in our lives, but would it give us what we wanted in our home? We would not be able to use the piece of driftwood I carried over many rods of portages on our canoeing and camping trip. I would have to pack away Sam's branding iron that I'd searched for all over western South Dakota. The antique duck decoy I'd bought at an auction would be banished from its place on the stereo to be replaced by a statue of Spanish dancers. The original pen and ink drawing of the Roman Coliseum, done by a friend of my parents as their wedding gift, would have made way for a new print of a Spanish castle. In all the houses I'd lived in as a child, we knew we were at home when that print went up over the sofa.

Suddenly these things became more precious to me than the most lavishly decorated room in the city. I would not allow this man to stifle our creative urge. I would not let him take from us the right to combine the new with the old. I would hold on to our heritage.

We left the store and went back to our old furniture. We placed my grandmother's rose bowl beside the two-foot candlestick made by a friend from an old cedar fence post. Our daughter's old doll cradle held magazines, and Sam's grandmother's worn sewing basket held my knitting. The leather strung drum that our son had made from a hollow tree trunk became a small table, and we found a place for the Coliseum print, even though it was not over the sofa. As for the furniture, it took on a new glow when we had it reupholstered that spring and moved it into new locations. And the specially cherished straight chair with bottom rungs obviously worn by little feet now had a new cushion—the chair that I had purchased from a friend for a quarter.

I knew we were right in our decision when the local home economics teacher asked me to allow her students to tour our house during their study on furnishing accessories. Had I remembered the salesman's name I would have written him. I couldn't even remember the name of the store!

None of us needs to remain in a poor condition. We may find ourselves in a certain condition today partly because of circumstance. But today each person can take hold of his or her life and refurbish it, turn it around. If I truly want to change, I can bring it about. I can begin to exercise and lose weight or improve my posture. I can decide to make positive actions to improve my personality.

Positive Action Choices
- What part of my life must I hold onto?
- What needs to be placed in a different perspective?
- What needs to be refurbished and made new?

Houses Along the Way

On my walk I saw a new house with a wide expanse of windows overlooking the lake. My dreams went wild with the possibilities of living in such a house! What a place to invite guests to sit and marvel over the beauty of God's world. And what a place for creative writing!

Is this my "passion" that becomes a temptation? How does it compare to the early Christians' passion for their previous pagan practices? Growing up in the Christian faith, I have no previous practices to steal my heart, but do I have other passions that have as great a pull?

And then I recalled God's commandment, "You shall not covet your neighbor's house." This brought to mind a theology I've held for some time, that God would not have needed to give us those ten great laws if we would only keep our wants and desires, and our thoughts and decisions, in line with God's plan for our lives at all times. Considering our common negligence, our tendency to stray from God's goal for our lives (some people might call it original sin), it's good that God did give us those Ten Commandments. They act as trigger points, not so much to "keep us good" as to draw us back to God.

As I walked down the path I realized that there are different houses for different people. Some people look at houses as simply a place to hang your hat and rest your weary bones. Others consider houses statements about themselves and about their lifestyles. And other people see a house as a refuge of comfort when the outside world becomes too much. Several years ago a friend needed to replace her roof. She decided to replace it with white tile, which is more expensive than tile of a darker color and considerably more expensive than a composition roof. When asked why she chose white, she said, "It makes a statement!" Sometimes we need to stop and reflect just what sort of statement our houses and our other possessions make to the world. Is the statement one of simply boasting? Is it one of welcome? Is it one that says I have pride in what God has given me, or in my heritage?

Houses and Statements
- Take a few minutes and walk slowly around your house. Write two statements that someone who doesn't know you might say about you by looking at your house.
- Walk through the various rooms of your house. Use your senses, and in each room list statements that come to mind about yourself and your lifestyle.
- Reread the statements. Is God reflected in these statements? Is the lifestyle reflected one that God calls you to? Are there areas in your home where persons (including yourself) can draw closer to God? Are there places that speak of community with others?

As a child I thought very little about houses. I grew up in parsonages, and I looked at a house as simply the place where we lived at that time. I recall that I couldn't understand why anyone would move into a different house unless they were moving to a different town.

I recognize now that the houses and their surroundings did have something to do with my formation. I never learned how to take falls easily because my parents didn't let me crawl on the splintery floors of an inner-city parsonage. I did, however, overcome some fear of heights as I swung from the trees around our home in south Georgia. I grew to appreciate water as I wandered for hours along two creeks that ran through our property when we lived in the outskirts of Tampa. And I learned to appreciate the labor that actually goes into the building of a structure when my husband and I built both a log cabin and a timberframe home in north Georgia.

In the twenty-five houses I've lived in during my lifetime, each has held a special significance to my life. Depending on what's going on in our lives at any specific time, our housing needs differ.

Before our last move, Sam and I considered prayerfully just what needs we would have in our new home. I felt God directing me to leave a full-time staff position and spend more time in writing and conducting workshops. Sam had retired six years earlier but had taken a full-time job at the local marina while I was employed full-time. With both of us leaving full-time employment, we knew that we needed to move into a home with lower taxes. Yet we needed room for my work as well as for guest space, since we often opened our home to people who need some Florida rest and relaxation. We had also learned that a bright and airy space enhanced my writing. And so with those thoughts we began to form some basic needs for our house. To determine the location, we knew that we must live in a neighborhood with families of all ages, and we looked at convenience to shopping, to an airport, to some places that give us spiritual renewal, and to our church (which we had already considered prayerfully). This list of needs simplified our search. It kept us from looking at homes out of our price range and in areas that did not meet our needs.

Through the years I've found that the way we view our homes and the objects in them can be very revealing. Try this exercise. Refer to the guide and examples that follow to write a cinquain (sin cane) poem about some part of your house. Your thoughts may be about a particular room or a piece of furniture. Whatever you choose, don't worry if your poem is not perfect. The creative experience of writing the poem will help to clarify that object's relationship to your life and to the direction that you see God leading you. We often forget how our calling or vocation is reflected in all areas of our lives.

In years past every household went through a spring-cleaning. I recall the story of a small log house just outside a little town where we lived in South Dakota. I never knew

---

Write a Cinquain

Line 1: A one word title or the object you're thinking of.

Line 2: Two words about the subject, either independent words or a phrase.

Line 3: Three verbs or a three word phrase denoting action. You may use words ending in "ing."

Line 4: A phrase or four separate words telling about feelings for line one.

Line 5: Repeat of line one or a word that explains line one.

Carpet
Unused. Welcoming.
Imagine the possibilities.
Furnishing makes it home.
Complete.

Life
Uncluttered. Receptive.
Canvas awaiting opportunity.
God holds the paintbrush.
Creation.

---

the woman who had lived in the house, and by the time I moved there the house was beginning to deteriorate. According to the story, when the owner was young, on the first warm day each spring, the woman took every stick of furniture outside. Then she would thoroughly scrub down the inside and outside of her little home, making it shine with the luster of the new spring day. I must admit that I never had the urge to do such thorough cleaning. In fact, with our frequent moves I seldom did thorough cleaning except when we moved into or out of a rented home. It was a jolt one day when I realized we'd lived in this particular house long enough that the walls and ceilings needed cleaning! As I cleaned them I saw that they were whiter than I'd remembered. By washing the grime away I brightened the house and everything looked different.

In all areas of our lives the grime builds up slowly over a long period of time. With the slow accumulation we become somewhat conditioned to the grime and fail to realize it must be washed clean. Perhaps we should automatically mark our calendars with periods to do physical and spiritual housecleaning. It would certainly brighten our lives in many ways!

I once read a book on organizing a household. The author suggested selecting one room each week to thoroughly clean. Perhaps a room a month fits your schedule better. Or perhaps you find scheduling a semiannual cleaning of the whole house more to your liking. Select a time when your calendar is less cluttered, or simply schedule it into your agenda. We usually function better in other areas of our lives when the home front is organized.

In the same manner, determine just what housecleaning your spiritual life requires. It may be taking time to read a book on prayer, or it may be purchasing a loose-leaf notebook and setting it up as a prayer journal. Perhaps you have several friends who need a note of encouragement, but you've not found the time to write. Set aside a regular time to attend to such matters and list items as you think of them during the week. By planning the time and making a list, you relieve yourself of stress.

Gardens and Growing Things

The garden along the lake set me to thinking about other gardens, some gardens that march in perfect rows, every similar plant together, and some gardens that are nothing but a few tomato plants in a flower bed and a row of lettuce along the fence.

There are also gardens like my dad used to grow, large

and varied. I remember one of his gardens took up a full vacant lot behind our house. When he had a few seeds left at the end of the carrot row, they filled out the turnip row that ran short. If a tomato plant died, he stuck in a few seeds of squash. The pumpkins seemed to beam like happy faces from the branches of the tree where the vines had climbed.

Bloom where you are planted.
Bloom wherever you find yourself growing.

As I stood before the garden along the lake, I recalled the driveway of the vine-covered garage. There, between the flat paving rocks, dandelions had taken root. This garden had no dandelions, yet the leaves of dandelions make a delicious green vegetable. Just why do we decide that certain plants are acceptable and others are called weeds? In north Georgia I discovered some of the most beautiful late summer blooms that I could have in my house were the huge mauve heads of the joe-pye weed. They grow profusely along the roadside, and although it has some medicinal powers, no one would consider having it in the garden.

Such thoughts on the ordinary bring questions to our minds. Do we sometimes treat persons like this? Do we automatically label them inadequate in some way, when in reality they have great value? Jesus accepted everyone, no matter what society said about them.

Even the scarecrow in this garden by the lake is a combination of discarded articles. The clothes are probably outgrown, or items with tears and holes. The old hat may have come from a storage closet, and the straw was probably some cast aside grass. Yet all of these items are reclaimed and serve a useful purpose.

The dark black humus of the dirt in this garden along the lake reminded me of the compost that my father tended for his garden. In Latin, humus means fertile ground. The dictionary lists it as the organic part of the soil that results from the partial decay of plant and animal matter. The earth takes our garbage and makes it into fertile ground. That's something like what God can do with our lives, no matter how rotten they seem to be. Perhaps this puts a different light on Jesus' statement, "Happy are those who are humble; they will receive what God has promised!" (Matt. 5:5 GNB).

And perhaps this is a clue to a simplified life. By allowing God to use our selves, by allowing God to take all parts of ourselves and re-create them into something useful or nourishing, then we receive that ultimate relationship with God. We simplify our direction: to be used by God.

Alleyways

In two places where I have lived we had alleys. I admit to being an alley walker. Now some people may think that an alley walker is nosy, but actually we're only people who enjoy nature in its natural state. The best place to find this in a city is along the alleys.

There are days when being an alley walker has its drawbacks. Those are the days that the garbage truck is due and is a little late. Or sometimes it's the day after someone's big fishing trip. Only the neighborhood cats like the smell of the alley then.

But most of the time alley walking is delightful. For one thing, everyone's more friendly in the alley. Even the dogs that bark at me when I walk by their front yards usually run up with wagging tails in the alley. Perhaps they're more accustomed to foot travel in the alley.

In an alley I may visit with someone I've never met and learn about making geraniums bloom. Then I'm likely to walk away with slips of the plant to root. Or I may stop to talk with a group of children and learn about their dirt hill city with miniature cars and pretend people. In one alley where I often walked, a mourning dove always greeted me from her television antenna perch. I could hear her mournful cry from blocks away, and the days she wasn't there I felt I was missing a friend.

Alleys offer a variety of nature. You will find everything from the perfectly manicured lawn to the tangled underbrush of a deserted house. And I must admit that sometimes the yards of tangled underbrush with their child-frequented tunnels look more refreshing than the manicured lawns. The tunnels invite you to crawl among the bushes and see just what lives there. They take me back to my childhood of roaming the tangled underbrush along the Florida creeks near my home. It was there that I first had a personal experience with God.

What are some alleyways that lead you back to your faith roots? What places and events today will help you recall those times?

Lake Source

On my walk around the lake, reflections on the water brought many thoughts of my own faith walk. Each aspect of the lake spun off to another vision of God.

Goldfish are interesting creatures. Goldfish are actually small carp. They will grow according to their environment. I kept a goldfish in a bowl in my office for six years, and it never got any bigger. Yet the goldfish in this lake are large, many of them ten to fourteen inches long. When they were released into the lake, they grew to their normal size. Perhaps our spiritual lives are much like that. As long as we content ourselves with a goldfish bowl theology, we limit our growth and swim around looking at the world from our own secure little environments. But when we venture into the lake of new ideas, we begin to grow and become what God intended us to be.

There is a phenomenon on lakes that thrills me every time I see it. Our family calls it "racing white horses." The horses seem to mill around over the water and then gracefully race across the surface, occasionally turning to race back again. In reality the majestic horses are only columns of steam being lifted from the warm, moist lake into the air currents above. Is this marvel of water transformation something like our relationship with God? We sometimes slide along the riverbed, keeping within the banks. At other times we bounce across rocks and problems, making for a rough ride but coming to an exhilarating climax. And there are also times when we find ourselves, like those "white horses," simply lifted above the surface, suspended in the currents of prayer.

At the end of the lake is a dam. Many years ago someone watched a small river flow through this valley and envisioned a lovely lake. It must have seemed empty when the dam was first built and the trees cut. Then the lake began to fill. As I look around I recognize that there are several drainages and small creeks that flow into the lake. Perhaps I should take a lesson here. Can I be more open and accepting to all the "filling water" that God brings into my life? Am I, as the lake, eager to receive from all directions? And do I willingly overflow and spill out for others? Or do I continue to build dams higher and higher, fearful of losing a drop?

As I approach the bridge that spans the outgoing water, I realize how this bridge unites the community on one side of the lake with the other. Like the bridge, God unites me with persons elsewhere. Some are folks I know and some are beyond my awareness. Some are living, some lived in the past, and some are yet to come. But each of us has the uniting experience of worshiping God.

From the creek behind my childhood home to our visits to the ocean, water has always lifted me spiritually. Unable to afford waterfront property, we have just finished creating a water garden in our backyard. Although our pond has no water feeding into it constantly, and although the water level sometimes lowers from evaporation, I'm reminded that we never completely use up the water. We move it around on this earth, and we manipulate our earth so that water is sometimes not accessible to everyone, and sometimes the water takes different forms. But every bit of water that was on the earth thousands of years ago is still here in one form or another.

Isn't God's power and God's love similar to that? Sometimes we accept it and spread it to others, sometimes we ignore God's call to action, and sometimes we see it in the smile or acts of another. But just as God promised in the covenant to Abraham, just as God celebrated over creation, that love and power is still here waiting for us to accept. Accepting is an act of worship, an act we can experience each time we watch for God in the people and things we encounter every day.

Chapter 8

FOLKS ALONG THE WAY

Having and Becoming Models and Mentors

As I reached the lake, there were several persons already making their way along the walkway. I fell in behind them, trying to match my steps to theirs.

As I reflected on my walk around the lake, I thought about persons whom I met along the way. Throughout my life, I have consciously or unconsciously decided whether to consider each person that I have met as a model for my own life. I may model parts of my personality after different persons, and I may at some point discover someone who stands out as the perfect model. We constantly try to match our steps with the steps of others who have walked before us, who walk beside us, and who walk out in front of us. But we must also realize that no matter how perfect a model someone may appear to be, that person is different. That person does not have the same genes, the same family background, the same life experiences as we do. Just as God didn't make us as puppets, so also God didn't make us as paper dolls, all stamped out of the same pattern.

Many years ago Charles Sheldon wrote a popular novel entitled *In His Steps*. In the novel a pastor challenges each person in the congregation to live life by reflecting on the question "What would Jesus do?" before they make any decision. This experience made a powerful difference in their lives.

Sometimes, however, we have difficulty placing Jesus into present-day situations, and it's easier for us to look to someone who is a present-day model of Christianity and ask ourselves, "What would that person do?"

Consciously selecting models can simplify your life

1. Select models who are serious Christians and who try to follow Christ's example in all areas of their lives.

2. Select models according to your own lifestyle and where God is directing you.

3. Measure your actions by how those persons would act.

4. Be open to finding new models when your course of direction changes or when a model's actions conflict with your goals or with Christlike behavior.

5. Constantly be on the lookout for new models.

We are not always aware that we are serving as a model for someone else. It can be very startling to discover yourself in this role, particularly when you are struggling with decisions in your own life. But recognizing that others look to you as a model can actually simplify your decisions.

In Romans 14:21 Paul advised the early Christians in their responsibility as role models. In their particular situation, Paul counseled them: "It is good not to eat meat or drink wine or do anything that makes your brother or sister stumble" (NRSV). For the Romans, the responsibility of being a role model was a matter of eating certain foods. For you it may be a way that you act or an attitude toward someone else conveyed in your speech. In all parts of your life, recognizing that others look to you as a model actually simplifies many decisions you will make by helping you to focus on how others will see and respond to your actions.

> *Recognize that others see you as a model*
> Ask yourself:
> "If I call myself a Christian, will someone else make the decision to follow Christ or not to follow Christ according to my actions?"

There are persons who may never know God without you. God came to Moses through a burning bush experience. Then God spoke to Moses about Aaron, his brother, and told him that although Aaron would speak for Moses, Moses would serve as God for Aaron (Exod. 4:16). You *are* the Bible for someone, the only Bible that person may ever know. Other Aarons will learn of God through you.

Searching out models and recognizing ourselves as models force us to look at our lives and reflect on God's calling. Mentors can help us to process that reflection. With the help of a mentor we can see ourselves as in a mirror. Both models and mentors can help to simplify our lives.

The term *mentor* comes from the Greek myth of Odysseus. In the myth, Mentor was Odysseus' loyal friend and adviser, and the teacher of his son. A mentor differs from a model in that the mentor is sought out and acts in a more personal way, consciously teaching and advising. The mentor is a guide or a resource person—someone who may not have all the answers but who is willing to help you search. The difference between a mentor and a model can be likened to a consultation and a seminar. In a consultation, you work with areas that affect your particular situation. In a seminar, the speaker covers a broad area, some of which may not apply to you.

Working with a mentor also encourages accountability. When you have a mentor whom you admire, who has helped you to set your direction, then your decision to follow the suggested course of action becomes simple. You know that your mentor will be pleased, and you know that the direction you set together will be helpful to you. You are eager to follow through. Accountability becomes an inner desire, not an outward constraint.

Often we are hesitant to ask someone to act as a mentor. Sometimes when we are going through a course of study, a mentor is assigned to us. But at other times we may need to seek out our own mentors.

Suggestions for Working with a Mentor

- Decide to pray for each other, perhaps at a specific time each day.
- Agree to be honest and confidential, recognizing that God loves in all situations.
- Discuss goals and the necessary steps to accomplish those goals.
- Set a timeline for accomplishment of each step.
- Schedule meeting dates to review and celebrate accomplishments.
- After each step, determine whether you need to reset your direction. Your goals or timeline may need to be adjusted. Evaluate the methods for meeting your goals.
- Hold each other accountable—you for completing the steps to achieve your goals and your mentor for resourcing, guiding, and encouraging you.
- Plan some spiritual enrichment that you will work on together. This enrichment may be reading a particular part of the Bible or a special book or article. Sharing spiritual growth will strengthen the relationship.

Models and mentors act as patterns and mirrors. Models simplify our lives by acting as patterns of the way; mentors help us look at the past, as in a mirror, and eliminate the need to labor over the past by responding to our specific actions and by helping us reset our direction.

Folks Who Block God

I remember the woman with earphones whom I almost bumped into on my walk. She had her thoughts elsewhere and blocked her surroundings from her mind. She wasn't aware of the missed opportunities to encounter God. Some folks run through life, filling their ears and hearts with what someone else has told them is good. They never listen to the many experiences that God puts before them.

Others, such as atheists, block God by their denial of God's existence. Just what is an atheist? According to the dictionary, an atheist believes that there is no God. Ask a person who claims to be an atheist why he or she doesn't believe. The atheist may answer, "Because God can't be like _____." Such an answer indicates that the person has actually formed an idea of God but does not feel comfortable confronting others with his or her idea. And so the atheist blocks God by denying God's existence. Perhaps rather than being an atheist, the person is actually rebelling against an idea of God that does not fit with his or her beliefs.

On the other hand, Psalm 14 warns about persons who voice a belief verbally but say "There is no God" in their hearts. These persons often profess popular words about God. But the words are hollow and their actions carry no meaning. They may quote every red-letter "Jesus word" from the Bible, but they don't live their Christianity. These persons often block God for other folks. Their unchristian actions turn many away from God.

How Do I Block God?

- Do I resist seeing the needs of another person?
- Do I hurry through life without hearing the birds or discovering the violets?
- Do I refuse to listen for God in other folks?
- Do I ignore the times that God gently spurs me to action?
- Do I fill my life with what others consider more important than God?

List specific times and ways that you block God:

_____

_____

_____

_____

_____

And a Little Child Shall Lead Them (Isaiah 11:6b)

Seldom do we realize how much we can learn from children. We think that we adults must always act as teachers. We feel that children are uneducated and must look to adults for guidance. Yet Jesus brought a small child into the midst of adults as an example. As the oldest child of a family with many children, Jesus must have had experience with little children and recognized ways that we can model our lives after children in order to recapture the joyful expressions that we have been taught to push aside.

During my walk around the lake, I saw the child's joy in feeding the ducks. This reminded me of studies on laughter. Children laugh an average of four hundred times a day. We adults laugh about fifteen times a day.* Laughter and other joyous experiences give us endorphins, and

* James E. Loehr, "You Can Do It, Too," *USA Weekend,* 15-17 July 1994, 5.

endorphins make a difference in our physical and emotional health. Research is only beginning to discover the benefits of endorphins.

How much joy do you experience on a daily basis? Do you need to become more childlike? Here are some questions to help get you started.

Think of These Things

- When was the last time that you really laughed until the tears ran down your face?
- When have you put everything on hold and enjoyed an adventure as when you were a child?
- When you take a vacation, how long does it take for you to forget about what's going on at home?
- How many times have you laughed in the past twenty-four hours? Count them.

Perhaps we need to make a conscious effort to become more childlike. Try some of these suggestions.

- Select a one foot square of ground and note everything you see in that square.
- Take a walk with no destination.
- Splash through the rain.
- Run in circles with a puppy.
- Investigate different items just to enjoy the texture.
- Hug a tree.
- Fly a kite.
- Ride a bike and enjoy the wind in your face.
- Walk barefoot and laugh as the grass tickles your toes.

More than anything else, learn to be like a child by using your mistakes and bad experiences to learn, rather than moaning over them. Past experiences cannot be changed;

they can only be used or cursed. Life is much simpler if we use past experiences.

Sharing the Load

It seems that throughout our lives we spend a lot of energy wishing that we were a different age. Young children look up saying, "Me too!" Soon they complain that they're not old enough to go to school. Then they don't want to go to school. Elementary school children can hardly wait to be in middle school, middle schoolers can't wait to be in high school, and high school students long for the day that they get their driver's licenses. Teens see twenty-one as a carrot dangling in front of their noses, and then within a few years they're wishing they were back in high school.

We view life differently at varying ages. The old man simply sat by the lake, observing the ducks from a distance as they worked the grasses under the water. When the toddler appeared on the scene, he approached the ducks, immediately grasping the opportunity to draw the ducks to him. He wanted to be a part of the action. Each attitude is important in life, and each generation brings new insights. We must look at things from all angles.

I've heard it said that God gives children to the young because they have the energy to keep up with them. Yet some of the most congenial relationships happen between grandchildren and grandparents.

Fifty years ago, most family members lived within short distances of one another. When children had difficulty communicating with parents, there was an aunt or a grandparent to whom they could go. When parents had difficulty with a headstrong child, members of the extended family acted as a support group. To an outsider, these relationships may have seemed complicated, but in reality they simplified life. Each person in the extended family was known for his or her specialty. You wouldn't think of going to Aunt Jane when you needed to know about what vegetables to plant because Cousin Helen had the green thumb. But if you had a problem with sewing, then Aunt Jane was your authority. Each person had his or her specialty, and no one had to be an authority on everything. No one was expected to be a Super Mom or a Miraculous Dad. With such a support system, each person excelled in something, and everyone shared the load.

Perhaps we need to find out more about our friends and acquaintances. Who excels in what? Are there some services and expertise that we can exchange? How can we share the load?

The Perils of Perfectionism

Folks are interesting! Some folks wouldn't step foot outside their door without every hair properly in place and appropriate attire, even for a walk down the driveway to pick up the paper. The man on my walk who greeted me as he picked up the paper was not embarrassed to be seen in his gray flannel bathrobe. He seemed relaxed and happy to greet the day.

Almost every time I move to a new community, I resolve to always make myself presentable before I go to the grocery store or a neighborhood shop. Then the day comes when I have only a few minutes to purchase something, or I'm rushing to the post office with a manuscript that must be in the mail before the post office closes in fifteen minutes. There's no time to do more than run a comb through my hair. There go my good intentions!

There is nothing wrong with good intentions and doing something right. In fact, doing things right the first time saves redoing them at a later date, thereby simplifying our lives. We can pursue excellence without becoming perfectionists. Long-range goals help us draw the line. Set your goals and periodically review them, adjusting them according to each new circumstance. Accept mistakes and look at them as opportunities to grow.

Life becomes complicated when we cannot be happy unless everything is exactly the way that we expect it to be. Life becomes even more complicated when we try to impose our standards on everyone else.

Perfectionism puts blinders on us. We spend our energy dealing with the frustration that life is not as we expect it, and we miss the unexpected that God sends our way.

According to J. Clayton Lafferty, who, with Lorraine Colletti-Lafferty, did a study on perfectionism for Human Synergistics International of Plymouth, Michigan: "Perfectionism is a way of thinking and behaving that, on the surface, seems a search for excellence . . . but (it) actually brings great unhappiness, massive imperfection, and poor health."

Are You a Perfectionist?

Read these descriptions and rate yourself from 0 to 3:
0 — never   1 — seldom   2 — sometimes   3 — always
____ I feel no matter how well I do, it's never enough.
____ I feel I must control or anticipate the future.
____ I'm disappointed after success, when I should feel good.
____ Others would say I'm too hard on myself and others.
____ I feel guilty when I'm not working.
____ I suffer from frequent headaches on weekends.
____ When I relax, I still think about work, or things I must do.
____ I dominate conversations.
____ I become extremely upset with standing in line, waiting in traffic, receiving poor service and with anything even slightly out of order.

____ Other people rarely live up to my high standards.
____ TOTAL

> Score yourself using the following scale.

0-5   You could hardly care less about being perfect.
6-10 You're not likely to have serious problems with perfectionism.
11-20 You have a tendency toward perfectionism and should be concerned.
21-29 You're on the troubled road of perfectionism, but a detour is still possible.
30   You're a perfect perfectionist, and probably feel perfectly miserable.

—Human Synergistics International*

Here Are Some Practical Tips for Perfectionists:

- Recognize that God made each person an individual with his or her own will, and the actions of others are out of your control.
- Set aside time each day to do something totally useless. Write this useless time on your calendar.
- At least once a week, intentionally laugh at a mistake you made.
- When reviewing a project, concentrate on the end results instead of parts of the process that may not have been as you wanted.
- At the end of the day, record your successes, even the smallest steps of success in a large project. Include such things as getting to the bus stop on time, giving a friend a word of encouragement, remembering to buy gas. Celebrate the successes!

* "Perfectionism Can Lead to Destruction," *Fort Myers News Press*, 17 November 1994, 12a. Reprinted by permission. © 1989 by Human Synergistics, Inc. All Rights Reserved.

- Make a point to listen to the other person's conversation. When possible, write notes about what the person is saying.
- Use waiting times to talk silently with God. Count the number of times you had such an opportunity to talk to God each day and look at those times as gifts from God.
- When you feel anger toward someone for mistreating you, flash a prayer to God for that person.

Stepping Aside for Others

On the dam at the end of the lake is a very narrow bridge. I recalled how the jogger and I stepped to the side of the bridge and watched the mother and children pass on their way to school. There comes a time in life when we must step aside to allow others to make their way.

Jesus told us that when we concentrate on gaining life, we lose it; but when we allow our life to be lost for others and for Christ, then we gain life (Luke 17:33).

Consider a handful of sand. If you hold the sand tightly, it escapes through your fingers. However, when the sand is held in an open hand, even when it is brimming to the edge, it does not escape. There is a time for clinging and a time for letting go.

Our parental relationships are sometimes the hardest from which to step aside. When the children are young, we parents hold the central focus of their lives. As they grow older, their peers become more important. But we still want to control their lives because we want them to live in such a way that they satisfy our needs.

When our children were in high school, we received an announcement that a psychologist would talk on peer pressure. We immediately put the meeting date on the calendar. When we arrived we found the room full of parents, all waiting to hear how our children were influenced by their peers. Were we ever in for a surprise! The psychologist announced that he was not there to talk about our children's peers, but rather about our own peer pressure.

We were reminded that fifty years ago families were larger—including four or five children. These large families usually had one child who excelled in sports, one who did well academically, one who had an outgoing personality, and one with talent in music or the arts. He pointed out that today most families have two children, but we still want a sports hero, a child on the honor roll, a child who is the most popular in class, and one who excels in music or the arts. This puts a lot of pressure on our two children, and it also puts pressure on us. We rush from soccer practice to dance lessons, from drama practice to band practice, and try to sandwich homework in between. When we learn to accept our children as they are, recognizing their individual talents and allowing them to develop their own direction in life, parents' lives become more simplified. We no longer feel pressure to have children who perform like the neighbors' children. In fact, we can even encourage our children to choose between options and set aside some free time.

Because we remove such overrated expectations, our relationships with our children improve. We also find that we have more time and fewer car pools! We must step aside and ignore some of our own desires, thereby allowing our children to become as God directs them.

The same holds true for all other relationships. A friend told me about her pastor who constantly enables others to take up Christ's ministry. She said that any time someone compliments him on an accomplishment he says, "It could not have happened without you (or without someone else who helped)." He showers the congregation with personal notes of appreciation. His affirmations enable each member to go the extra mile. By stepping aside and passing the praise on to others, he becomes more effective and the church becomes stronger.

Sometimes we can enable others by simply planting a seed of an idea. Once it takes root, the origin of the idea may be lost. Although the person may come to believe that it was his or her idea, you can recognize a pride within yourself that you planted the seed. God knows how the idea came about, and in the end that is all that matters. Stepping aside actually simplifies your life. The mission is accomplished, and you don't have to do the project yourself. Take pride in enabling others.

Some Steps in Stepping Aside

- Be alert to others' dreams, and look for opportunities to help them fulfill those dreams.
- Before taking on a project, think about persons to whom God has given talents that would be useful in that particular situation. How can you involve them in the ownership and planning of the project?
- Plant seeds of ideas and allow others to water and reap the fruit.
- Record persons who enable your successes, and offer a prayer of thanks.
- Recognize accomplishments by others and write notes of appreciation or make calls to them.
- Sincerely, but simply, acknowledge compliments given to you.
- Include others when receiving credit for an accomplishment.

To paraphrase Jesus' statement, when we step aside and remove the limelight from ourselves, we grow in our ability to carry out God's mission. We also become models of Jesus' life.

Along the path, we continually try to match our steps with the steps of others who have walked before us, who walk beside us, and who walk in front of us. We find models all around us, and we are each a model for someone else. We search out mentors on whose shoulders we may view the world. And we simplify our lives by recognizing Christ in folks along the way.

Chapter 9

RESTING AWHILE
Worshiping God

*As the pathway climbed a little hill I
began to wish that I hadn't passed up the
opportunity to rest. . . . Now that I needed
a break, there was no bench in sight.*

How typical of me to pass by the opportunities for rest.
And then once I decided to rest, I looked for a bench when
actually a rock worked as well. And how typical of us all,
to pass by opportunities along the way to worship God.
We must worship God in spirit and in truth, not just in
buildings and potluck dinners, as well as in sermon
preaching and book writing.

Worship has been defined many ways, because worship
is different for each person. We should be thankful that we
cannot understand God. We must only encounter God. If
we knew everything there is to know about God, then
God would not be God. We would have no reason for
worship, for we can only worship that which we cannot
fully understand. Yet in our struggle to better understand
God we arrive at new revelations, at opportunities to say
"Aha, *there* is God!" Each new "aha" becomes an experience of worship.

What makes our worship of God even more exciting is

when we recognize that, although awesome and undefinable, God is personal and concerned about each of us. As Jesus said, even the hairs of our heads are numbered. Such a God who is beyond our comprehension also cares enough to know when one hair comes from my head. God cares enough to know that I've found another gray hair or that I may be balding.

Moses met God in a burning bush. When Moses pondered God's assignment for him and questioned whom he should say sent him, God gave him the word *Yahweh*, which means "I am who I am." We try to define and label God and become frustrated. We experience or encounter God who knows and loves each of us personally, and become free.

Words for Worship

Many people have used many words to describe worship. Spend a few moments reflecting on each of these words. What images or experiences of worship does each word call to mind? What additional words can you add to the list?

happening **marvel** *cheers* lift up

transformed happiness *praise* **YES!** **ENCOUNTER**

release concern **RESPONSE** celebration

experience involvement **love** **SURPRISE**

joy reverence *amazement* wonder

awe

A Personal God

I recall sitting in a worship service as a child and listening to the patriarchs of the church wax eloquent prayers, sprinkled with *thee*'s and *thou*'s and other majestic words.

At that time God seemed far and removed from me. My literal mind placed God in human form, far above the earth and looking down on all that we did. As an adult, I learned that the language of the King James Version of the Bible (where we got our *thee*'s and *thou*'s) was quite different from our language today. When the King James Version was written, the words *you* and *your* were reserved for formal situations, and *thee* and *thou* were only used in a very personal way, primarily with family and those they held dear. Today we have completely reversed the language.

In reality, God is a very personal God. God comes to us in a family sort of way as the greatest, most loving, most caring, most understanding parent that there could ever be. One time when our adult daughter was having a particularly difficult week, she called us saying, "I want to be a kid again!" I've had that feeling myself, a desire to relinquish my problems, to let someone else handle them, and simply to release myself into the loving arms of a parent. Such a personal God we have! God acts in the most affirming parental way, reaching out with loving arms so that we may rush wildly into them. As you experience the image of those arms close around you, feel the peace entering you, moving through your veins and throughout your body. Don't worry about how to make yourself at peace, just accept it, knowing that it's there.

Peace I leave with you; my peace I give to you. I do not give to you as the world gives. Do not let your hearts be troubled, and do not let them be afraid. (John 14:27 NRSV)

Spontaneous Worship

It was a crowded mall, and I rushed on my way with an armload of packages. I could think of a host of ways I'd rather spend my time than shopping. I even had to wait my turn for the escalator. As I stepped on the bottom step I began to click off a mental list, checking to be sure that I had everything I needed. Suddenly, I focused on a child looking over the shoulder of the woman in front of me. There was a hint of a smile around his mouth that then curled his lips. I automatically smiled back, and his eyes flashed with joy, lighting up his whole face. In that child I saw God, in the midst of a crowded mall, at a time when I'd rather have been somewhere else. I will probably never see the child again, and he will never know that he helped me to encounter God. It was one of those spontaneous moments of worship, a time when I knew there was a personal God. One of those times when we say to God, in the enthusiastic way of youth, "*Yes!*"

These spontaneous opportunities abound throughout our day. We encounter them everywhere from the shopping mall to the rock by a quiet lake; from the sanctuary of a church to the shower stall at home. But we must look for these opportunities. We must watch in order to see the small rabbit under the squash leaf. We must use our inner eyes in order to see God in the lacy spiderwebs on the bridge, heavy with last night's rain and sparkling in the sunlight like jewels on a queen's robe. Throughout the day if we open ourselves to God's anointing presence we can grasp those worship moments.

We need to look for the bloom hidden under the leaf, recognize the power of a fragile bird's wing, wonder over the creation of an infant, and appreciate the way God put our noses on our faces so that we won't drown in the shower! It's these small opportunities that nourish us and simplify our lives. They center us on God, again and again throughout the day. By drawing us back to God, we again recognize our central goal, which is to live according to God's plan. All the problems and frustrations now begin to fall into place.

Experiencing Peace

We also must set aside times for experiencing solitude or peace. What concepts does the term "being alone" bring to your mind? Rejection? Unpopularity? Being a wall-flower? Or does it signify creating an empty vessel to be filled by God?

Richard Foster reminds us that "The movement inward comes first because without interior transformation the movement up into God's glory would overwhelm us and the movement out into ministry would destroy us." *

Solitude nurtures simplicity. There is a difference between solitude and isolation. Isolation implies being cut off from others involuntarily. Solitude is by choice. Positive spiritual growth can come when we choose to spend some time apart from others and with God. Since it is our own choice, then we recognize that after our experience of soli-tude we can move back into relationship with other per-sons, stronger from spending such time alone with God.

Likewise, there is a difference between private prayer and prayer in solitude. Private prayer shuts others out so that we don't have to deal with them. Prayer in solitude draws us apart so that we may hear God and know better how to deal with and help others. One is a selfish attitude of prayer and the other is an outgiving attitude, seeking direction through prayer.

> But I have calmed and quieted my soul,
> like a weaned child with its mother;
> my soul is like the weaned child that is with me.
> (Ps. 131:2 NRSV)

Instead of the hungered frenzy of a nursing child searching for food, we can be calm and quiet with God,

---

* Richard Foster, *Prayer* (San Francisco: HarperSanFrancisco, 1992), 6.

not begging and demanding, "Give me, give me!" but being simply content to accept God's love.

> *Quietness and solitude produce the fruits of the spirit. It is out of that quietness that we become the fruit that reflects God's image, as a child reflects the parental image as he or she matures.*

Finding Our Sabbaths

One of the commandments that we often ignore is, "Remember the sabbath day, and keep it holy." The Sabbath comes around every seven days.

Seven is a significant number in the Bible. My concordance records almost four hundred times that the number seven is used in the Bible. God is pictured as creating the earth in six days and then resting on the seventh. Twice Noah waited seven days between sending out the dove. Jacob served seven years for Rachel, not once but twice! Joseph forecast seven years of plenty and seven years of famine. The Hebrews celebrated the Passover by eating unleavened bread for seven days. They were to count seven weeks of seven years (forty-nine years) and then prepare for the year of jubilee, a year of celebration and rest. Every seventh year the Hebrews were to grant a remission of debts. The feast of booths lasted seven days. Joshua led the Israelites around the walls of Jericho seven times, as they blew seven trumpets. The crops were to be rotated and the land left fallow every seventh year. Jesus broke seven loaves of bread with the fish to feed the crowd. The law said that a person should forgive seven times, but Jesus said seventy times seven.

The number seven seems to be a natural cycle. God made us with a need to rest. The details of how we must rest are not as important as the necessity of that resting time.

When I was a child the accepted way of resting on the Sabbath was to avoid physical work. My mother considered herself liberal when she allowed me to do needlework (which I found to be very relaxing) on Sunday. When I was in college I struggled over how to observe my Sabbath. For six days every week I labored mentally. We even had classes on Saturday mornings at my college. Many of my classes were religious in nature. On the seventh day, the last thing I wanted to do was tax my brain! I taught a second-grade class on Sunday mornings, and the most rewarding Sabbath afternoons were usually spent doing some sort of physical labor, even cleaning my room. I actually found myself praising God as I swept the floor and rearranged furniture. This Sabbath brought the needed interruption in the routine. It was a natural break in the cycle. The physical labor brought a balance to my life.

Many of us who work in the church on weekdays and then again on Sunday must find another Sabbath. What is your plan for a Sabbath? When can you break the rhythm and find a new approach to God?

Breathing and Praying

Our pauses for refreshment along the way cannot always be planned. In fact, sometimes they can only be squeezed into those narrow spaces of time. But there is always time for worship, for prayer.

In the book *When I'm Alone*, Ron DelBene suggests using a breath prayer.* Quite simply, this is a prayer that may be said in one breath, breathing in and out. What follows is an adaptation of the steps outlined in his book.

* Ron DelBene with Herb and Mary Montgomery, *When I'm Alone*, 7-9. Copyright © 1988 by the authors, published by The Upper Room. Used by permission of the publisher.

1. Make yourself comfortable and quiet. Close your eyes. Remind yourself that God loves you and you are in God's presence. Recall a favorite poem or passage of scripture, such as "Be still, and know that I am God!" (Ps. 46:10).

2. Imagine that God is calling you by name. Listen carefully and hear God asking , "(your name), what do you want?"

3. Answer God with whatever comes honestly from your heart. Use one or two words or a short phrase in the answer, such as "Peace" or "I want to feel your forgiveness." If several ideas come out, combine or focus so that you find a specific need that is as basic to your spiritual well-being as water is to life. Ask yourself: What do I want that will make me feel most whole? Peace of mind and peace of heart will follow wholeness.

4. Choose a favorite name for God: God, Jesus, Christ, Lord, Spirit, Creator.

5. Combine your name for God with your answer to God's question "What do you want?" This becomes your breath prayer. It may be "Let me know your peace, O God," or "Jesus, I need to let go of troubles." Try placing God's name at the beginning and at the end. One way may feel more comfortable than the other. Change the words as needed so that the sentence flows smoothly, as in a breath. Now say or think the words of the prayer as you breathe in and breathe out. Write the prayer down and use it several times during the day—in fact, any time you think it. Soon it will become a part of your life.

Torrents of Water

As I watched the thundering waterfall from the bridge, I realized that a force of power flowed from the lake. Several small streams brought the water to the lake from many directions. The streams flowed quietly through the streambed, moving around rocks, rising to higher levels at times and barely trickling at other times. At the waterfall, the water, after being held in the arms of the lake, spilled over the dam in a torrent.

Is my life like this waterfall? Or is it like a child's water pistol? Both use water. Both must be filled. But one is capable of generating great power and being useful to other people. The other is capable only of generating aggravation. The waterfall is God-given power, like God showering us with love at our baptism. The water pistol must be powered by another person, and it only puts out a little squirt.

We must choose between the inexplicable power of God, filling us as we dwell in the Scriptures and live day-by-day in communication with our God, or the periodic power of other people, a source refilled only according to their interests. Just as the lake is filled by several stream sources, so we are filled when we dwell in the Scriptures, study devotional materials, and surround ourselves with models and mentors. Then we lie in loving arms, as we take time to worship and live day-by-day in communication with our God. My choice of a power source comes as I look to God's direction and decide that God's choice for my life is my choice.

When we rely on the power of the waterfall, on the inexplicable power of God, we receive the capacity of transferring that power to others. We become the transformer that carries the power to others. We do this through caring acts, through sharing our understanding of God, and through praying for other people.

The choice is there. Will we constantly struggle to satisfy other people's expectations, or simply look to God for our power and direction? By choosing God, acknowledging that guidance, and receiving the waterfall of power, our lives are simplified. We move on down the river, refreshed and able to spread God's love to those along the way.

I must choose the baptism I want. I must voluntarily step under the waterfall instead of waiting for someone else to squirt me with the water pistol.

Taste and See

As I rested against the rock on the lakeshore, the tender tip of the prickly brier vine brought back memories of walks in the woods during my childhood days. Picking the tip had been automatic, something I've done for years each time I've encountered the prickly brier. I thought of the significance of the thorny vine. It may have been such a vine that was used to make a crown of thorns for Christ at his trial. Only the tough, hardened vines with rigid thorns would have worked to form a crown. The men tormenting Christ would probably have thrown away the new, tender shoots that could have been used for nourishment.

When we simplify our lives, when we bring order to our material possessions and time schedules, when we look for God in the ordinary and in other people, when we worship God, then we choose to take the tender shoots instead of the rigid thorns. By selecting that which is nourishing, we accept Christ instead of piercing him with thorns. Experience God and taste the goodness.

Sometimes in our rush we eat without tasting. In the past few years, Sam and I have seldom eaten out. One evening, however, as I returned from volunteering at our local hospital, Sam greeted me at the door with a suggestion that we eat out. With the excitement of children we pulled out a coupon book we had purchased and decided on a restaurant we'd never tried before, one that no one had told us about. Then we set off for an adventure! To our delight, the food was delicious. In fact, it was so good that I decided to eat very slowly in order to savor its flavor over a longer period of time.

There is something about tasting that changes the rest of the body. Instead of going out to the restaurant, we could have gotten the same amount of nutrition from a glass of water with protein powder and a couple of vitamin pills. But the experience of tasting each piece of meat and each vegetable brought nourishment to our whole being, not just our physical body. We savored the taste and remembered it for several days afterward.

I remembered the young boy who was feeding the ducks along the edge of the lake. His mother took the bread and broke it, giving pieces to the boy. The boy ate some, fed some to the ducks, and shared some with the older man.

The boy took what he had, what had been given to him. He received nourishment from eating it, and he also received nourishment from sharing the bread.

How like our eucharist. We accept what is given to us. We receive nourishment, both physical and spiritual, and we share that with others. For celebrating communion would never be the same if not shared with others.

Jesus was a great experiential teacher. Look at how he used the common elements of bread (the most common food of his day) and wine (the most common drink of his day, even more common than water). He used what was at hand and turned it into a real understanding of how we must make God a part of us, internally, in order to be whole, fulfilled, and satisfied—to be physically and spiritually complete.

A friend of mine tells of when she was a teenager and first recognized the significance of the symbol of taking the bread and wine (or juice) into our bodies. She was told that through this act, we actually take Christ into our bodies to be a part of us. Suddenly the thought came to her, "Well, Jesus, what does it feel like to be a girl?" Oh, that we all could feel close enough to God to speak in such a familiar way! To literally feel that Christ has become a part of us! The young shall lead us.

Communion

Christ became bread for us,
    to be "eaten up" by us,
        completely giving of self.
We become bread for others—in our own circumstances,
    to be "eaten up" by others,
        completely giving of self.
This brings the simple life for those who become one with
  God.
This is how they are immersed in the faith and find joy.
    And this is how we may also find joy.

● ● ● ● ● ● ● ● ● ● ● ● ● ●

Edward J. Farrell, in his book *Gathering the Fragments,* speaks of Jesus taking us, blessing us, breaking us open, and passing us around. An interesting thought.

Chapter 10

AFTER THE WALK
Looking Ahead

With the refreshment of a shower and the memory of my walk, I turned to face the day. I knew that God and I could deal with anything that came my way!

And so my walk came to an end. I took the wilted rose petals from the rose garden and laid them out to dry. Memories to muse upon after I left the lake. Memories to carry me through the year. How will the walk make a difference in my life? How could the walk make a difference in your life?

When you live in search of material possessions, you reach for a high standard of living. When you search for God in your life, you reach for a high standard of life.

> *High standard of living*
> *vs.*
> *High standard of life*

Like the hermit crab that walks out of its shell and finds another more fitting to its maturity, we are free to change our shells. I don't know where it came from, but I remember the first lines of a poem I often used when I was in high school. It went something like this:

> I've made up my mind to be happy,
> I've been gloomy and glum long enough.

It is amazing how one's attitude can change when we simply decide to change! Isn't this really the heart of prayer? We can change only ourselves, and others change as we interact with them. The change in others comes through God, as we allow God to change us.

Paul wrote to the Philippians: "Whatever is true, whatever is honorable, whatever is just, whatever is pure, whatever is pleasing, whatever is commendable, if there is any excellence and if there is anything worthy of praise, think about these things . . . and the God of peace will be with you" (4:8-9 NRSV).

Playing the Tune

The many facets of our lives are like an orchestra.

When they do not function together
    —do not follow one orchestra director
then there is disharmony and chaos.

But when each area of our lives is tuned
    —and sometimes this takes time apart from others
then our whole life plays a true tune.

The tune may be complex.

It may be sad, or it may be happy
    —but no matter what, when directed by God,
then it is true.

Like the Magi who worshiped at the manger, we encounter Christ and then return by a different road. Our lives are simplified because we walk the simple walk, following God's road map.

Remember that simplicity begins on the inside. If we strive for an outward lifestyle of simplicity without first developing the inward reality, then we have legalism much like the Pharisees of Jesus' day.

As you develop your inward reality, follow God's direction and use the following action plan and checkup to work on simplifying your life externally. These will not give you simplicity of heart, but they will prepare you to receive it.

Without pausing for reflection, check in the left-hand column the items you want to try. Add other goals that may come to your mind. Mark a date on your calendar, six weeks in the future, to go back over the list and see how many of those items can be checked in the center and right-hand boxes. Remember that it takes six weeks of continual practice to change a habit.

Thank God and celebrate those items that you have accomplished! Enjoy the pride of accomplishment. Spend time in prayer, asking for any new direction that God may have for your life. Then look at the remaining items and determine what action may be necessary to follow God's direction. Use those items, and any other actions you need to accomplish, to make a new action plan. You will never arrive at a perfect plan, because you are constantly changing as the circumstances around you change and as God's plan for your life unfolds. Set aside a time every six weeks to review and renew your plan and continually seek God's guidance for your life.

Action Plan and Checkup

Date begun _____ Date for six-week review _____

I'll try	I do usually	It's a habit!	
☐	☐	☐	Check refrigerator for leftovers daily.
☐	☐	☐	Choose simple, healthy foods such as fresh fruits and vegetables over convenient foods such as doughnuts and pizza.
☐	☐	☐	Request removal from direct mail advertising lists: Direct Marketing Service, 6 East 43rd St., New York, NY 10017.
☐	☐	☐	Use postage-paid envelopes of advertisers to object to unwanted advertisements.
☐	☐	☐	Adjust family attitude toward allowances: train to manage money.
☐	☐	☐	Practice recycling.
☐	☐	☐	Walk rather than drive when I can.
☐	☐	☐	Clean house, asking "Do I really need these items?"
☐	☐	☐	Think a prayer for every person I meet each day.
☐	☐	☐	Find ways to own items cooperatively or enjoy without owning.
☐	☐	☐	Try giving items away, anticipating the freedom this will give me.
☐	☐	☐	When considering purchase of a gadget, decide if something I already have will do the job.
☐	☐	☐	Make celebrations home-centered, not purchased entertainment.
☐	☐	☐	Entertain because I want to (genuine hospitality), not to impress.
☐	☐	☐	Switch to cloth no-iron napkins, fabric shopping bags, and so on.
☐	☐	☐	Set water heater at lower temperature and install timer.
☐	☐	☐	Budget television time, deciding on positive shows.
☐	☐	☐	Discuss items advertised on television as necessities. Can we live without it?
☐	☐	☐	Make a game of commercials, recognizing manipulation.
☐	☐	☐	Coordinate local trips/errands to save gas and time.
☐	☐	☐	Make attending worship a weekly habit for me and my family.
☐	☐	☐	Prepare for Sunday morning the night before.
☐	☐	☐	Resist contests and "free" prizes.

I'll try	I do usually	It's a habit!	
☐	☐	☐	For three to seven days before doing it, think about purchasing an expensive item or making a major decision.
☐	☐	☐	Set aside regular times to be alone with God.
☐	☐	☐	Plan a way to serve others (as a family) at least once a month.
☐	☐	☐	Keep a record of where our money goes.
☐	☐	☐	Contribute to the church on a regular basis.
☐	☐	☐	Select a routine event (mowing, driving, changing a diaper) and find a way to make God the center of that act.
☐	☐	☐	Set little goals (instead of one large one) and rejoice when each is accomplished.
☐	☐	☐	Set aside time for myself periodically.
☐	☐	☐	Look for God in everything around me throughout the day.
☐	☐	☐	Prioritize my time each day.
☐	☐	☐	Practice active listening.
☐	☐	☐	Remember to laugh more each day.
☐	☐	☐	Call upon family and friends for support when appropriate.
☐	☐	☐	Enjoy leisure time without thinking about work that needs to be done.
☐	☐	☐	Read and meditate upon God's Word on a regular basis.
☐	☐	☐	Be conscious of ways I model for others, and of others who model for me.
☐	☐	☐	Find a mentor to work with.

Selected Bibliography

Books

Brother Lawrence. *The Practice of the Presence of God*. Nashville: The Upper Room, 1950.

Broyles, Anne. *Journaling: A Spirit Journey*. Nashville: The Upper Room, 1988.

DelBene, Ron. *Alone with God*. Nashville: The Upper Room, 1984.

Dunnam, Maxie. *The Workbook of Living Prayer*. Nashville: The Upper Room, 1974.

The EarthWorks Group. *50 Simple Things You Can Do to Save the Earth*. Berkeley, Calif.: Earthworks Press, 1989.

Foster, Richard. *Celebration of Discipline*. New York: Harper & Row, 1988.

_____. *Freedom of Simplicity*. New York: HarperCollins, 1981.

_____. *Prayer*. New York: HarperCollins, 1992.

Hall, Douglas John. *When You Pray*. Valley Forge, Pa.: Judson Press.

Job, Rueben, and Norman Shawchuck. *A Guide to Prayer for All God's People*. Nashville: The Upper Room, 1990.

Weatherhead, Leslie. *The Will of God*. Nashville: Abingdon Press, 1972.

Webb, Lance. *The Art of Personal Prayer*. Nashville: Abingdon Press, 1977.

Periodicals

alive now! (devotional bimonthly magazine), 1908 Grand Ave., P.O. 852, Nashville, TN 37202.

Weavings (journal of Christian spiritual life), 1908 Grand Ave., P.O. 852, Nashville, TN 37202.

Study Guide

Prior to Session 1, give out copies of the book and ask persons to read the introduction and chapter 1. As you prepare to lead each session, read the chapters completely, but ask participants to read the chapters covered *after* each session. Stress the importance of reading the chapters after the group discusses the material in order to make this a part of their life each day.

Session 1 (covering chapters 2 and 3)
1. Participants draw/select a picture that reminds them of happiness.
2. Share pictures. Talk about difference between happiness and joy.
3. Use meditation on gift from page 17.
4. Discuss information on pages 19-24 concerning God's will.
5. Take *Lifestyle Inventory* test (pages 25-26).
6. Review Bible study and prayer suggestions on pages 30-37.
7. If time allows, study Matthew 12:43-45 using method on page 31.
8. Lead group in "Why Do We Love?" on page 38 and close with prayer.
9. Ask the group to read chapters 2 and 3.

Session 2 (covering chapter 4)
1. As they arrive, have participants do "A Money Autobiography" on page 43.
2. Summarize material on pages 41-44.
3. Read Matthew 6:19; 19:24; and Luke 6:30-31, 34; 12:15, 33; 16:13; and 1 Timothy 6:10.

4. Review questions on page 45 and then, in pairs, discuss items that are signs of unnecessary or ostentatious elitism today, like the braided hair and elaborate robes mentioned in 1 Peter 3:3 were signs in the early church.
5. Summarize material from the bottom of page 45 through page 47.
6. Take inventory of essentials on page 47.
7. Review "Wise Purchases" on page 48 and summarize remainder of chapter.
8. Close with litany prayer, asking persons to mention items from the inventory list (page 47) with responses: After "essential item," group responds: "Thank you, God, for supplying needs." After "would be nice" item, respond: "Make me a good steward."
9. Ask the group to read chapter 4.

Session 3 (covering chapter 5)
1. As participants arrive, ask them to draw a large clock on a piece of paper and to write inside their clocks everything they did yesterday, from brushing teeth to signing a contract.
2. Read 1 Peter 1:13-16 and then pray prayer on page 53.
3. Do exercise *Evaluate Your Activities* on pages 55-56.
4. Summarize information on pages 56-57.
5. In small groups, do Bible study suggested on page 58.
6. Point out suggestions on pages 58-60 for later reading.
7. Complete checklist on page 61.
8. Ask for suggestions of ways to experience joy in life without expense or extra time. (For added ideas, see "Alternative Joys" on page 63.)
9. Close with prayer using the participants' suggestions for joy.
10. Ask the group to read chapter 5.

Session 4 (covering chapters 6 and 7)
1. As participants arrive, ask them to list all of the persons that they recall encountering yesterday. They may not know the names of every one.

2. In small groups discuss: How do you feel when asked to be silent and listen without offering comment? How do we normally use words to control, manage, or convince others?
3. Summarize information on pages 66-74.
4. Silently look at names on list (see number 1 on previous page) and pray for each person.
5. Divide participants into groups and assign each group a spontaneous experience with God in chapter 7 to read and reflect on, then the groups will share their thoughts with the total group.
6. In groups, take four routine events (mowing lawn, driving car pool, cooking dinner, swimming) and illustrate how you can make God the center of each.
7. Share these ideas with total group and close with prayer, thanking God for the ordinary.
8. Remind the group to read chapters 6 and 7.

Session 5 (covering chapter 8)
1. As participants enter, ask them to be thinking of someone in their life that was instrumental in their faith—who helped them know God better.
2. Bring everyone together in a circle. Using a ball of yarn, pass the ball back and forth across the circle, asking each participant to mention the person instrumental in his or her faith, wrap the string around a finger, and pass the ball across the circle to someone else. This creates a "web."
3. After everyone has shared, talk about how we all touch one another's lives and are connected by a web of relationships, just like the yarn web we created. Pray a prayer of thanks for those who have touched our lives.
4. Summarize information on models and mentors on pages 89-92.
5. Divide into small groups. Give each group a large piece of paper and markers. Ask group members to illustrate times that they have seen children worship, or when children were in awe of God. (Examples include watching a

butterfly, seeing a new sprout from a seed, or taking communion.)
6. Read Isaiah 11:6*b* and Matthew 18:1-5 and review pages 94-95.
7. Ask each person to think of one way he or she will become more childlike this week.
8. Summarize pages 100-103.
9. Close by reading Luke 17:33 and by asking God to help us to act as models.
10. Remind the group to read chapter 8.

Session 6 (covering chapters 9 and 10)
1. Review *Lifestyle Inventory* test (pages 25-26) and record changes participants have made.
2. Write the words for worship (page 106) on individual slips of paper and place them in a basket. Ask each person to draw a word from the basket and tell about images or experiences that the word calls to mind.
3. Pray a prayer of thanks for the many experiences of worship. Close the prayer with the words:

We cannot understand you, God. If we understood you, then you would not be God. We can encounter you, however. With each opportunity of worship we arrive at a new revelation, finding times we can say "Aha, *there* is God!" To Moses you said, "I am who I am." Thank you for being the *Yahweh* of Moses, and the God of each of us. Amen.

4. Review *A Personal God* on pages 106-8 and ask participants to share some time of spontaneous worship they experienced in the past weeks.
5. Summarize *Experiencing Peace* and *Finding Our Sabbaths* on pages 109-11.
6. Hand out a calendar page for the month you are in or for a new month that is soon to begin. Ask participants to fill

in events they can remember and then to write in a half day somewhere that they can set aside for God, for reading and reflecting. This will be a Sabbath.

OPTION: Select, as a group, some time in the next few weeks to come together for a half day retreat. This would be unstructured, and participants would bring their own reading/reflecting materials or use reading materials you would have available.

7. If time allows, have participants fill out the "Action Plan and Checkup" on page 120. If there is no time, point it out to them and ask them to fill it out in the next twenty-four hours.

8. Use format under *Breathing and Praying* (page 111) to help participants develop a "Breath Prayer."

9. Remind the participants of the sacraments of baptism and communion, using some ideas on pages 112-16. Then, if possible, close with the sacrament of communion as a group.

10. Ask the group to read chapters 9 and 10.